How I Got Over

Clara Ward and the World-Famous Ward Singers

How I Got Over

Clara Ward
and the World-Famous
Ward Singers

Willa Ward-Royster,
as told to Toni Rose

Foreword by Horace Clarence Boyer

TEMPLE UNIVERSITY PRESS
Philadelphia

TEMPLE UNIVERSITY PRESS, PHILADELPHIA 19122
Copyright © 1997 by Temple University. All rights reserved
Published 1997
Printed in the United States of America

♾ The paper used in this book meets the requirements of the American
National Standard for Information Sciences—Permanence of Paper for
Printed Library Materials, ANSI Z39.48-1984

Text design by Gary Gore

Library of Congress Cataloging-in-Publication Data

Ward-Royster, Willa, 1922–
    How I got over : Clara Ward and the world-famous Ward Singers /
Willa Ward-Royster : as told to Toni Rose : foreword by Horace Clarence Boyer.
        p.   cm.
    Includes index.
    ISBN 1-56639-489-9 (cloth : alk. paper)
    1. Ward-Royster, Willa, 1922– 2. Gospel musicians—United States—
Biography. 3. Clara Ward Singers. I. Rose, Toni, 1934– . II. Title.
ML420.W183A3   1997
782.25'4' 092
[B]—DC20   96-5943

Contents

Foreword

*T*HERE ARE SOME persons or groups upon whom falls the responsibility—sometimes joyous and sometimes painful—of creating, developing, and refining a concept, practice, or style. As a reward or punishment for that labor, they become the standard imitated or shunned by those who follow. For female Gospel groups that honor goes to the ensemble from Philadelphia that has been known variously as Gertrude Ward and Daughters, the Consecrated Gospel Singers, the Willa Ward Singers, the Clara Ward Singers, and, most widely, the Famous Ward Singers.

The Ward Singers were not the first Gospel group, of course. There were male Gospel groups: The Foster Singers had been organized in Bessemer, Alabama, in 1915; the Fairfield Four in Nashville, 1921; the Harmonizing Four in Richmond, Virginia, 1927; the Dixie Humming-birds in Greenville, South Carolina, 1928—and these were all still very popular in the mid-1930s. There were also mixed groups. The Bertha Wise Singers—an all-male group of five who, following the path of the annual National Baptist Conventions, sang early Baptist-style Gospel throughout the United States—had inspired, for example, Roberta Martin's (1907–69) and Theodore Frye's (1899–1963) Martin and Frye Quartet (Chicago), which changed its name to the Roberta Martin Singers in 1935. There were all-female groups as well: As early as 1926 the blind Texas-based pianist and singer Sister Arizona Dranes (c. 1905–60) was assembling occasional female (as well as mixed) backup voices for her recordings of sanctified Gospel. And Thomas Andrew Dorsey (1899–1993), the "Father" of African American Gospel music, sometimes used an all-female trio or quartet to demonstrate his songs—though he preferred soloists such as Sallie Martin (1896–1988) and Mahalia Jackson (1911–72).

In 1934, however, when Gertrude Ward (1901–81) celebrated her third year as a Gospel singer in her first anniversary concert, advertising selections by "Gertrude and Daughters," there was no other permanently organized female Gospel group. But Gertrude had no need to consider basing the group's style on that of, say, one of the already established male quartets; she had ideas of her own. As leader of the group, Gertrude Murphy Ward was one of the most original personalities in Gospel. With surprisingly fine-tuned intuition and ambition, she set about creating a female Gospel group persona. (Indeed, four of the other five major female groups of Gospel's Golden Age, 1945–65, that took shape in the next decade were, in part, inspired by the Wards: the Sallie Martin Singers and the Original Gospel Harmonettes in 1940; the Angelic Gospel Singers in 1942; and the Davis Sisters in 1945. The fifth group, the Caravans, did not organize until 1952.)

Employing the natural voices of her two daughters, Gertrude placed Willa (b. 1922) in the first soprano range. She chose second soprano for herself and assigned Clara (1924–73) a high alto part. The three voices produced a light and lyrical sound that was capable of cascading, with ease, into the upper register of the female range. Willa served as the original accompanist for the group, but "Little Clara," as she was called in those days, soon adopted some of the technique of the sanctified pianists, and the sisters began to share that responsibility. Each of the three doubled as soloist and harmonizer, and the Consecrated Gospel Singers, as they were soon called, began to perform at churches throughout the tri-state area of Pennsylvania, New Jersey, and Delaware and on into the Southeast. Gertrude knew that there could be a professional musical life in their future and chose the 1943 National Baptist Convention as the venue for their national debut. With Clara playing the piano and leading one of the old Baptist lining hymns so dearly beloved by this congregation, the Wards became the sensation of the convention.

Under Gertrude's aegis as manager and booker, the group was soon traveling as far away from Philadelphia as Buffalo, New York, and Anderson, South Carolina, Gertrude Ward's home. On occasion, substitute singers would be brought in, especially after Gertrude had a goiter operation that changed her voice and left it unreliable. Two such singers were Henrietta Waddy (1902–81), a South Carolinian like Gertrude, and Marion Williams (1927–94), a Floridian. Waddy possessed a rough and unsophisticated low alto, but she was able to blend with the pure voices of the Wards. She was a powerful leader of "jubilee" (moderately fast) and "shout" (very fast) songs and a very physical singer. Williams possessed an extraordinarily refined, high lyric soprano but could essay her lower range without difficulty and growl with the best of the Baptist preachers. Brought up in a Pentecostal church, she was well grounded in "shout" songs at very fast tempos, using fill-in words at points where the melody called for a rest, repeating words and melodic motifs for intensity, and singing with unusual volume. (Later, in 1958, Marion Williams, Henrietta Waddy, and three more recent members of the Ward Singers—Kitty Parham, Esther Ford, and Frances Steadman—formed a group of their own called the Stars of Faith. Eventually, Williams left the Stars of Faith to embark on a solo career.)

With Clara as lead singer and arranger, the Famous Ward Singers not only defined the female Gospel sound but set about establishing the demeanor of the female group in performance. They walked into an auditorium or church straight and proud like movie stars, formed a line across the stage close to the piano, and, because they knew their material so well, did not even look at one another as they burst into song on the same beat, with the same enunciation, same volume, same nuance, and same beauty. In the early days they wore regular church robes but soon adopted elegant suits or dresses, which quickly gave way to elaborate sequined evening gowns. To complete their dramatic image, they often wore coiffured wigs, and they would make their appearance in towns from Philadelphia to Los Angeles in a long Cadillac with a trailer attached. Not only did they sing beautifully; they were talked about— exactly what Gertrude Ward wanted and needed in order to turn her singers into superstars.

Although the Ward Singers began recording hit singles in 1947, it was not until 1949 that they had their biggest-selling hit, their first gold record. That October they recorded W. Herbert Brewster's (c. 1898–1987) "Our God Is Able." Clara completely reworked the song, dividing the lead between Williams and herself and adding call-and-response sections at the beginning and the end. After a five-note introduction, Clara sings the word "surely" twice, with the group repeating; then they sing the first verse in harmony before moving into the chorus, in which Clara takes the lead. Using the same melodic motif and the same accompaniment in the background voices, Clara rehearses miracles worked by God in the Old Testament: "He was Moses' bush burning; He was Solomon's Rose of Sharon; He was Joshua's mighty battle ax." Williams introduces the second chorus with one of the Ward Singers' trademarks, the "high who," which was created and popularized by Willa. This device involves drawing out the word "who" on a high note and is usually employed when moving from one chorus into another to present a seamless fabric of sound. Williams begins it while the other singers are completing the preceding chorus and holds it for seven full beats, then goes on to detail what Jesus will do for those who follow Him—"He'll be your friend when you are friendless; He's a mother for the motherless, a father for the fatherless; He's your joy in sorrow"—and concludes with the word "surely" (Williams pronounces it "showly") repeated several times, each time with a group response. "Surely, God Is Able" (to which Brewster changed the name of the song) became one of the biggest hits in Gospel and was sung by choirs and local groups throughout the nation.

Among the Ward Singers' other hit records, "How I Got Over" established Clara as a singer extraordinaire. In this journey to heaven she spells out the trials one must experience in order to reach the Master, followed by a litany of gratitude that begins with thanks for parents and goes all the way to thanks for "ole time religion" and "a heavenly vision." Another popular Ward Singers recording was "Packing Up," again with Williams celebrating the "high who."

Recordings and successful concerts placed the Ward Singers in the forefront of Gospel music. Not only in demand throughout the African American church community, they began to receive invitations from the likes of Ed Sullivan, the Newport Jazz Festival, and comedian Jack Benny. Eventually, Gertrude and her singers went on to wow audiences in Japan, Clara went on to play Las Vegas and star in a Broadway play, and Willa went on to lead her own group at Radio City Music Hall.

Gertrude was a true entrepreneur, not only increasing the number of Ward Singers but creating a second group in 1951, which she called the Clara Ward Specials. This group traveled with the Ward Singers on double-billed concerts and also appeared in their own concerts, from which Gertrude received a percentage. During the course of her career, Gertrude formed numerous groups, including an all-male chorus. In 1953 Ward's House of Music opened in Philadelphia, publishing and selling Clara's songs as well as those of Brewster and other composers that the Ward Singers featured in their concerts.

Clara and Gertrude eventually settled in California, and the celebrity of the Ward Singers soared. The big time afforded them diamonds, furs, Cadillacs, and television appearances. Clara purchased an expensive home and amassed a coterie of stars as friends. She was seen and photographed at clubs, openings, and celebrations. Unfortunately, as Clara's popularity rose, her health declined, and in 1967 she suffered a stroke. When, unexpectedly, Clara recovered completely, she was hailed by many as the "Miracle Girl," selected by the Lord through His healing to carry His word throughout the highways and byways. After some years, Clara fell ill again. This time the end was near, and in 1973 the great Clara Ward, the musical inspiration behind the rise of female Gospel groups, succumbed to a second stroke and died.

After some forty years of fame as leader of the most successful female Gospel group in history, Gertrude immersed herself in the dwindling membership of a church Clara had purchased for her. She expected their complete trust and financial as well as spiritual support, but it was only a few years before money problems led to the loss of both the luxurious home Clara had left and the church Gertrude Ward so dearly loved. Gertrude attempted to organize other singing groups, pursuing her fading dreams, until she too became ill and passed away in 1981. The end of an era was at hand.

The story of the Famous Ward Singers has a sensational quality not normally associated with people who are affiliated with the Christian religion, or at least not until recent days. Willa Ward has not shied away from telling the candid tale of the Ward family's history. She has told not only a moving but an honest, revealing, sometimes shocking story—almost a Gospel "Mommie Dearest." Those who read the book will be titillated by its sensationalism but should not forget that at one time the Ward Singers were a symbol of all that was innovative and inspiring in black Gospel and that perhaps Clara is even now in heaven singing "How I Got Over."

Horace Clarence Boyer, author of
How Sweet the Sound:
The Golden Age of Gospel

Preface

HE WARDS' PATHS have crossed those of such a host of people that no matter how many Willa remembered, we knew we had omitted others. To these people we say, "Thank you for adding to the Wards' life tapestry."

What may seem like name-dropping for name-dropping's sake is really much more than that. Two contrasting scenes are important to the story. First, three frozen females standing waist-deep in snow before a deserted church whose door bears a crumbled sign, "Program Canceled." Second, world-famed supertalents standing in line for a Ward Singers' performance or eagerly sharing the same stage with them. It takes a lot of names to show how Gertrude and Clara and Willa got from one to the other.

Willa and I were so tempted to include a lot of sensational tales (naming more names), but even though such tales *might* sell more books, it is not our intention to expose or humiliate anyone. We believe the historical value of Willa's memoir and the fullness of its protagonists' lives are stronger selling points than revealing gossip would be.

We hope that when you see religious singers on television or join them in church or listen to their recordings, you will think of the Gospel pioneers. Every time the Holy Spirit surges through you and you tremble to a soulful rendition, every time you feel a shout coming on, every time an inspired voice moves you to tears—think of that forceful innovator Madam Gertrude, the divine Clara, the phenomenal Willa, and all the other Ward Singers. Think of how their vocal brilliance and their unequaled legacy have changed the Gospel music experience forever.

Toni Rose

How I Got Over

Clara Ward and the World-Famous Ward Singers

Prologue

*I*N 1931, Gertrude Murphy Ward, pressing clothes in a Philadelphia dry cleaning store, heard a voice: "Go sing my Gospel and help save dying and lost men and women." And again, standing on a street corner with other dayworkers, she heard the same voice: "Gertrude, sing my Gospel. Why look for another job when I've already given you one?" From that day on, Gertrude said, she "had no other job but to sing for the Lord."

In 1934, Madam Gertrude Ward celebrated her first anniversary as a gospel singer, and with her appeared her two daughters, Willa and Clara Ward, ages thirteen and ten.

By 1970, policemen had to control overflowing crowds for the Clara Ward Singers' concerts at home and abroad. In the meantime, Clara's mother Gertrude and sister Willa were on the move with their own groups. As one news commentator put it, "That's some kind of busy." And there was more to come.

This is the story of Gertrude and Willa and Clara Ward—the original Ward Singers and the leaders of the various vocal ensembles that performed under the Ward name for more than half a century.

Part One : 1901–1949

*T*HE YOUNG Murphy brood—all ten of them—huddled on the porch of the family's rural abode near Anderson, South Carolina. The larger children used their heft to get up front, flush with the door, and pressed their ears to the sun-bleached wood. The little guys did their best to penetrate the tangle of slender brown legs and faded coveralls.

In the room on the opposite side of that door a crackling fire neutralized the spring chill, yet the three occupants felt anything but comfortable.

Sweat and steam dampened Jessie Mae McDugal's body like soft rain as she stirred the rags being sterilized in boiling water over the fire. Inwardly, Jessie Mae was a cool, deliberate, and experienced midwife. For the drained man sitting on a milking stool by the bed, it was a different story. Dave Murphy was sweating in nervous anticipation through the long and difficult labor his woman was experiencing. A very pregnant Hannah Murphy was drenched, by now, after hours of excruciating pain.

It was April 19, 1901, and getting late in the evening when the baby's head appeared. Hannah grunted and pushed; Jessie Mae McDugal gently pulled and consoled; Dave Murphy paced the floor and praised the Lord.

The Murphy children squealed, hugged, and danced with delight when they heard the strong wail that was Gertrude Willa Azalee Murphy Ward's first solo.

Gert was just getting old enough to enjoy being the baby of the family when another baby came to slide her out of that favored position. The twelfth child was a boy named David. The Murphys' plentiful homegrown workforce was kept busy with farm chores. Chickens needed feeding and plucking. Cows had to be milked and taken to pasture. Wood was gathered for fires. In the spring, the ground was plowed by Dave and the older brothers, then raked and furrowed by Hannah and the younger children so that seeds could be planted. A new outhouse trench was dug. Lord knows, the old site had to be covered. A winter of daily offerings by fourteen people pretty well necessitated it.

Summer produced not only crops to pick, pickle, and preserve but abundant weeds and pests to dispose of. The Murphys were sharecroppers and had a fairly large tract of land to tend, most of it planted in cotton. Everyone picked. Sometimes they picked all day and ate lunch in the field. Songs helped break the monotony and take their minds off aching backs. One person would begin and then the others would join in, harmonizing or counterpointing. Some verses often humorous, were created on the spot.

The fall was a hectic yet happy time. Although the days were crammed with chores, some hours were always squeezed out for fellowship and merriment. For example, when animals were to be slaughtered and smoked, neighbors would gather together at one farm and all pitch in. Then, in the late afternoon, the celebration would begin. A huge fire illuminated the area and showed off the tables laden with mouth-watering country cooking. All the families contributed. Occasionally the men ambled off to the barn or some other designated spot, returning mellower and happier. Everybody knew they were drawn by that powerful magnet—good corn liquor.

Jokes and stories were popular, and one storyteller would try to top the other; you could hear the singing and laughter way up the road. When jokes about "Mr. Charlie and ol' Sam" (master and slave) evolved into tales of the not too distant past, however, emotions often sagged heavily between jollity and anguish. Accounts of the "worser than now" days puckered brows as if crimped by a rough drawstring. Mouths that had opened wide in mirth narrowed to tightly clenched wedges; lips were caught by the teeth to control the quiver. Every adult had a bitter ingredient to add to the memory cauldron: "Yeah, pickin' crops, if you missed a worm you had to eat it."

Mindful of letting the "young blood" know how it was, blacks at such gatherings all over the South shared almost identical stories. Stories of a father's flight from armed white men and baying hounds, while his trembling offspring crouched in their mother's arms. Stories of false accusations too often backed up by the white accuser's gallery of friends. Some whites, of course, put their reputations or lives on the line for blacks. In slavery days they supplied escapees with safe houses, food, contacts, and transportation. Some owners also broke the law by teaching their slaves to read and write, even though discovery meant severe punishment for both races. In these instances, whites had all to lose and nothing to gain except righteousness. Many of us would not exist if our foreparents had not been aided by a few gallant Caucasians.

Once the oldtime stories—good and bad—had run their course, someone would invariably pull the crowd back to frivolity. Some came willingly; others lingered in the decomposing sadness, but such evenings generally ended on a note of gaiety.

Church attendance was another frequent activity among the Murphys and their neighbors, for the churches provided collective strength and social as well as religious release from daily problems and everyday drudgery. Folks outside the experience may be unaware of the fervor of Baptist services. Bible passages read by a deacon or assistant pastor are commonly repeated and expounded upon at length by the regular pastor. He admonishes his hearers with threats of burning in hell for the sins of lying, drinking, fornicating, gambling, or disobeying any of the commandments God gave to Moses. He may begin his sermon in a slow, deliberate voice, then artfully modulate the intensity and tempo until his listeners are aroused to ecstacy. Almost every sentence is permeated with shouting and moaning from the congregation, each member contributing his or her own, seldom varying expression such as "Well, well," "Um-mmm," or "Preach it!"

Preachers adopt various styles. The singing preacher may introduce, accompany, and end his message with songs to create a mood of joy or sorrow or repentance and to wrest passionate responses from his flock. The healing preacher calls on the power of God to mend and cleanse the body and mind of a sufferer, usually transmitting the divine energy by the "laying on of hands" and repeated entreaties. Whatever the style, something mystical envelops the worshippers. Weak, strong, bold, or timid—all leave conscious posturing behind and "get the spirit"; they may speak in tongues, scream, faint, laugh, cry, or dance. The unbridled spontaneity of "getting happy" is the chief joy that some have in life.

Christians in the South worshiped the God of the Bible and loved Jesus, but some also relied on the voodoo conjurer or "root doctor" to remove spells or illnesses that they believed were brought on by evil forces, or to "fix" (place a spell on) another person or turn his evil work back on him. Root doctors, male and female, worked with herbs, grave dust, shells, dolls, fingernail parings, eggs—even animal sacrifice. Equally fearful were their maledictions and supernatural incantations, rituals that combined African and Catholic elements with inspiration from the "forces." We need to remember that all societies and religions have aspects and practices that outsiders find strange. Walking on water, raising the dead, and parting the sea are not everyday accomplishments either.

Gertrude and the other kids trudged almost ten miles to attend the Ebenezer Baptist Church, a one-room structure that was also the schoolhouse. There the teacher had her hands full teaching all the grades. The big boys were responsible for keeping the fire going in the stove. The other children had the task of collecting wood.

The end of the school day was welcomed by all. It was great fun to imitate the way the elders talked and walked. Gossip was just as juicy then as it is now, so it was on practically every day's menu. The walk home also provided the opportunity for courtships. A boy named George Ward really had eyes for Gertrude. Time would prove that she found him attractive, too. They had shared many warm moments by the time they finished eighth grade and left school.

Meanwhile, John, James, and Foster Murphy, Gert's older brothers, were becoming good musicians. They derived their music and lyrics not only from material they picked up at minstrel and traveling tent shows but from life experiences. Prisoners working along the roads and railroad tracks or busting rocks were the source of some of the more poignant songs in the Murphys' blues repertoire. Other tunes often had no words, just sounds borrowed from animals, wind, raindrops, saws being pulled through wood, train whistles and wheels running on the tracks—even lovers' utterances at the apex of passion. The rhythmical gestures of women working over washtubs was further inspiration; the *wu, sha-wu, sha-wu* of their knuckles on scrub boards evolved into the crisp, deeper tones produced by the strumming of masculine, work-hardened fingernails. (Do you suppose jug playing began with men long-sipping the homemade alcoholic joy the jug held? When your palate and lips get happy, there is a strong possibility you might want to get creative.) Soon the Murphy boys were skillful enough on banjo and fiddle to be in demand as party entertainers. The local white folks used their talents quite often. Payment varied; they never knew what or how much it would be until it was handed to them. Although cash was what they liked best, chickens and hams and the like were what the boys brought home most frequently.

One family that hired the Murphys consisted of a spinster, her two widowed sisters, and their grandfather. The local gossip was that the sisters were trying to snag husbands and used the parties as showcases for their culinary abilities. After playing for these three women and their guests one night, the Murphy boys came home later than usual and—what was worse—they were empty-handed. When Ma Hannah questioned them about the missing payment, her boys stammered and stuttered that somewhere between the party and home the money was lost, so they had retraced their steps in an effort to find it.

For days afterward, the boys found a lot to whisper and giggle about. The other kids had their own suspicions, as did Hannah and Dave, as to what had really happened and what the actual payment was—it most certainly wasn't anything that could be brought home. The boys' parents warned them never again to come back without something to show for their efforts. The older Murphys were concerned about more than the loss of payment. They knew that as willing as party guests might be to mix it up, such a mixture could prove to be deadly (literally).

In the room just off the porch of the Murphy home, where Dave had witnessed so many births, he experienced the other end of life's spectrum. The Murphy children's father died of a cerebral hemorrhage that left the floor stained with his last physical offering—a small precious pool of dark red blood. The year was 1918.

After the death of her husband, Hannah spent long hours rocking back and forth in her old chair, by now as comfortable as an old friend. The worn porch creaked in unison with the antiquated rocker. Sometimes she sat in silence, sometimes humming a spiritual over and over again, but always clutching and drawing on an old pipe whose bowl was almost burnt through. Each puff sent up lazy curls of smoke that seemed synchronized with the half-sighs, half-whimpers that emerged from a spot between her throat and her empty, broken heart.

One by one most of the Murphy children married and some migrated to the North. The preferred location was Philadelphia, Pennsylvania. By this time George Ward and Gertrude Murphy had decided to share their lives and to bid Anderson, South Carolina, farewell.

HEN AMERICA entered World War I in 1917, the government needed more manpower both to fight overseas and to fill jobs in defense plants at home. Blacks were encouraged to sign up for military service. Good money drew others (male and female) to the industrial North: Henry Ford's assembly plant in Michigan, the steel mills of Pittsburgh.

And then there were those who had a burning desire to be part of the musical excitement spreading out from New Orleans. Early on, Charles "Buddy" Bolden was mixing ragtime with jazz—that wild new music taken to the heights by innovators such as "Kid" Ory, King Oliver, Freddy Keppard, "Jelly Roll" Morton, and Louis "Satchmo" Armstrong. The saloons, brothels, bistros, dance halls, and even funerals were jumping. Soon this new music and its players migrated to Chicago's Storyville, where everything was wide open. The Illinois Central Railroad's line from New Orleans through Memphis and St. Louis to Chicago was carrying a lot more passengers north than it brought back.

After the war, black servicemen returning from Europe who landed in New York could not believe that shocking, delightful city. What would soon be known as the Harlem Renaissance was plump with sweet promise. Harlem's multifaceted population included poets and writers (Jessie Fauset, Sterling Brown, Claude McKay, Countee Cullen, James Weldon Johnson, Langston Hughes), intellectuals (Jean Toomer, Walter White, W.E.B. Du Bois), musical stage performers and playwrights (Nobel Sissle, Eubie Blake, Bert Williams, Ethel Waters, Paul Robeson), other musicians and singers ("Mother of the Blues" Ma Rainey, "Express of the Blues" Bessie Smith, Duke Ellington, Cab Calloway, "Fats" Waller, Fletcher Henderson). Even earlier, many had been drawn to Harlem by the civil rights organization that in 1910 became the National Association for the Advancement of Colored People (NAACP), formed to address the social, political, and economic ills that plagued all blacks. Added to all that, the returning soldiers noted, wealthy blacks were wearing fashionable clothes and jewelry, riding to soirees in shiny new cars. The discharged servicemen could hardly wait to tell the homefolks about all these wonders—or to find a way to come back. Unfortunately, the Big Apple's fascination blinded many of them to the down side: the poverty and hopelessness of those languishing in the silt of the ghetto.

Philadelphia, George and Gertrude's choice, was known as a "friendly city" to blacks (the protest of German Quakers against slavery as early as 1688 had eventually led to passage of the nation's first state abolition law). They lived throughout the city—not so clustered as in other urban areas—and many had profitable businesses. Until the Depression of the 1930s there was work for everyone who wanted it.

Philadelphia was also a city of churches and home to many of the oldest and most prestigious black congregations. The African Zoar Methodist Episcopal Church, founded in 1794, was chartered by the

Commonwealth of Pennsylvania in 1837, and in 1852 it hosted the first Convention of Local Colored Preachers and Layman. St. Thomas African Episcopal Church was founded in 1787 by a former slave, the Reverend Absalom Jones. Mother Bethel African Methodist Episcopal, the oldest A.M.E. church in America, was founded in 1787 by Richard Allen, who intended it to be open to all races.

Others include Enon Tabernacle Baptist Church, organized in 1878 at West Coulter and Tacoma; Mt. Zion Baptist Church, 1890, Rittenhouse Street near Germantown Avenue; Bethel A.M.E. Church, 1859, East Rittenhouse and Morton; St. Barnabas P.E. Church, 1904, Rittenhouse and McCallum; St. Peter Claver's, 1892, a black Roman Catholic congregation. The First African Baptist Church, established c. 1800 at 16th and Christian and later moved to 10th and Cherry, organized the Mutual Aid Insurance Society and later founded the Cherry Building and Loan Association and the school now known as the Downingtown Industrial and Agricultural School. The present Tindley Temple, begun in 1902 as East Calvary Methodist, was renamed for the Reverend Albert Tindley, its founder and a prolific composer of Gospel songs.

Some of these and many others would play a large part in the Ward Singers' career.

GERTRUDE'S sister Clara and her husband, Hamlin Burton, had already established a comfortable and ample home in Philadelphia by the time Gertrude and George arrived. They opened their abode to the newcomers without hesitation. Soon after moving in with Clara and Hamlin, Gertrude Willa Azalee Murphy changed her status and name. She became Mrs. George Ward. Before long the newlyweds were anticipating the birth of a child. Unfortunately, the baby miscarried.

Soon thereafter, however, came the little girl they named Willarene.

She was followed by a cute little boy. Father George was proud to have a Junior. He hoped for and envisioned things they could share as time developed the tiny body and expanding mind.

When baby George was about six months old, he became quite ill and was taken to a doctor, who prescribed a deadly treatment. Junior's temperature had risen to a dangerously high level. The good doctor, in all his professionalism, told the Wards to take the baby home, bathe him, and then put him near an open window to reduce the fever. In this instance the cure was worse than the illness. The fever was indeed broken, but so was the life line of little George Ward Jr. The next morning Gertrude cradled in her arms a cold, lifeless baby boy whose little face was washed with a grieving mother's tears. The death certificate read, "Cause of Death—Pneumonia."

A year and a half later, joy came again to the Wards. This time, it was a girl—a sweet little bundle they named Clara Mae. Little did George and Gertrude realize how greatly their two girls, Willa and Clara, would influence the family's future.

This early account has been told to me, Willa, by members of my family. From here on, the story is from my own memory, observations, experiences, emotions, joys, and disappointments—except where I had to aid my poor ol' brain by tapping other sources to get dates and names right.

*W*E LIVED at many addresses, but the first home I can remember was at 1218 Harper Street in North Philadelphia. Both our parents had jobs to make ends meet. My father was working at the Link Belt Company, which smelted iron and manufactured hardware of all sorts. He started there when he first moved to Philadelphia in 1920, rose from common laborer to foreman, and kept that little title until he retired in 1962. My mother did housework for a Mrs. White, who quite conveniently lived across the street from us. It's a good thing Mom didn't have to pay carfare to the job, as she made only thirty-five cents for an entire day's labor—although after a year Mrs. White gave her an appreciated fifteen-cent raise.

At about three, Clara was quite small, but she played and ran right along with me. She could run as fast as I did because my legs were still recovering from a severe case of rickets I had developed as an infant. My aunt told me I had been left in the high chair for many hours at a time, and nutritional deficiencies played their part as well. I had worn leg braces for several years. The three-and-a-half-year span between Clara and me thus made little difference. We played Mom and Pop and baby along with the other kids on the block, and had great fun darting in and out of vacant buildings and lots.

On the corner was the Strand movie house. We would go around and sneak in the back door. We were so excited and awe struck by the movies that it was all we could do to stay silent and protect our presence. Our favorite was the latest *Tarzan* film.

There were cousins living across the street, who were really fun to pal around with. In fact, our block was loaded with relatives. There was Uncle Charlie and Aunt Mattie, Uncle Dave (related to Mattie—not the South Carolina Uncle David) and Aunt Lugretta, cousins Harold, Charles, and Lunell and cousins Lovey, A.D., and Manson.

My parents had a Victrola that provided all of us with lots of fun. I dearly loved the latest popular records, and the kids on the block taught me all the current dances. And dance I did—for anyone who would watch. At that time, Clara couldn't have cared less for any of it. Although Mom enjoyed the music, we were not supposed to dance to it or sing it. Little did she know I learned to sing every song on every record. My expansive repertoire grew from that early time.

When my mother left the room, all the other grownups encouraged me to sing "Tight Like That." I had no idea what the lyrics referred to until years later. I guess the big kick was seeing and hearing me perform a risqué number in my totally innocent and ignorant fashion. How could I possibly know that the man who wrote that song, Thomas A. Dorsey, was the same Professor Dorsey who wrote a skit that Clara and I later performed in church, in which the entire dialogue was composed of gospel song titles.

Clara and I loved the holidays, and we had the joy of believing in Santa Claus. The very idea that someone so mystical cared enough about us to bring toys at Christmas was wonderful. We just loved the guy. We were especially ecstatic one Christmas, after we had been "playing" the windowsill as if it were a keyboard, when Santa brought a toy piano. We plunked that thing to death. Although I had learned to read notes in school, I couldn't play an instrument, but I sure played at playing the ivories. We pretended to be turning sheet music for each other. The one playing would swing her arms back and forth with such gusto, she would almost lose balance, but would manage a graceful sway on the up and down swing. The page turner always put quite an artful effort into that as well. We couldn't have played harder at a real concert.

A few years later, during one of several times we lived with Aunt Clara and Uncle Hamlin, the one thing that had us mesmerized was their lovely player piano. Hamlin and Clara's son, James Burton, played piano, vibes, guitar, and organ, and Clara and I loved to listen to him. But the big thrill was when he put one of the many popular music rolls in the player piano. We watched in awe as the keys magically depressed and all the wonderful music poured out. This was really our first introduction to the mechanics of piano playing. We memorized the key depressions in sequence and practiced them so that, in time, we could play some of the simpler tunes. When we picked out melodies by ear, though, we played only on the black keys.

When we weren't playing with and on the piano, we enjoyed annoying the family cat. One day, when the cat got annoyed with *us* and balked, we decided to teach it a lesson by shutting it in the closet. But that was no fun, so we tried to regenerate some interest by chasing the poor creature with a broom. The action got really lively and eventful. I got scratched by the cat, the kerosene heater was knocked over, a small fire erupted, Mom exploded, and our butts were darn near shredded.

*B*Y CHANCE, one day, Mom bumped into a friend of long standing whom she hadn't seen in quite some time, a Mrs. Corrine and her daughter Elsie. They talked of many things, including days gone by, and from that extended conversation came a shared address for our two families, in the 2300 block of Mervine Street.

This three-story building had large windows that greedily inhaled sunshine and released it into huge square rooms. Elsie and her mother rented the third floor, while we took the second (I don't know who was on first!). Usually, after dinner, we'd all go up to the top floor and sing Gospel songs. Sometimes the adults would sing so long and ardently that tears would stream down their cheeks. We kids would be caught up in the spirit, too. We sang, clapped, and sniffled without really understanding the emotions soaring through us.

Since all our parents worked during the day (much to our delight), we small fry crammed our unchaperoned time with explorations of our childish whims and fantasies. One day Clara, Elsie, and I scampered up to the third floor to carry out our plan to skate on the side of the building. We raised the windows as high as we could and proceeded to climb over the sills. The idea seemed workable until we put it into operation. Elsie and I were hanging on by our arms and fingertips, rolling the front wheels of our skates up and down the face of the building, when poor little Clara started to yell and slip. "Oh God, she's going to fall," I thought, but getting myself back in and over to her window proved far more difficult than anticipated. I finally made it just in time to pull a screaming pavement-bound sister over the hump. Elsie needed a little help, too; she was starting to panic. When we were all safe inside on the floor, we hugged, cried, and laughed together in nervous relief. We unanimously agreed to eliminate that caper from our repertoire.

Christmastime still filled us with great joy and expectation. We started talking early in the fall about what we wanted "Sandy Claws" (as Clara called him) to bring us. As the weather got cooler, we'd get magazines and papers out of the trash to line the cold steps so we could sit on them, and a picture in one of the magazines immediately caught my eye and fancy. This most divine piece of furniture I had ever seen provoked a desire I hadn't known before, a longing to possess something other than a toy or food. I couldn't wait till Mom got home from work to show her the picture of this gorgeous rolltop desk, and I put in my request that very day for Mom to let Santa know, if he brought me the desk I'd never ask for another thing. Boy, was I disappointed to be told he didn't bring things like that to children.

In December, we were frantically compiling our lists so that Santa would have enough time to get all our stuff collected. We must have changed our requests fifteen or twenty times. Clara's most desired items were new skates, dolls, and a baby buggy. I wanted new skates, a matching cap and scarf, and books. I didn't put the desk on the list because I didn't want old Kris Kringle to get all worn out looking for something as unusual as that and wind up too tired to bring anything—so I stuck with the more probable selections.

Imagine my complete surprise and utter delight to discover a beautiful roll top desk next to the Christmas tree with a bow and tag that read "Willa." For the first time, I didn't participate in the ritual of running in and out of houses and up and down streets with the rest of the gang, proudly showing and viewing all the new goodies. Instead, after my dad pushed it to the spot it was to occupy, I spent most of the day examining and admiring my new desk. By evening I had all my books and papers in their proper place. Great joy! Meanwhile, Clara had put miles on her new buggy, and her doll was already a seasoned traveler.

Three months later, when I came home from school with the intention of putting my books on my desk, I discovered an empty space where it had stood and my belongings stacked on a chair. The payments had never been met, so the supplier had come and picked it up. My heart was broken. That was also the first connection I made between Santa Claus and creditors.

*N*EVERTHELESS, old North Philadelphia provided us with some warm and lasting memories. We didn't realize at the time how rich and surprisingly self-contained these neighborhoods were. Corner stores—grocery, hardware, clothing, furniture, dry goods, drugstore—were usually owned by Jewish or Chinese people who lived above or behind their places of business. Newspaper stands, an icehouse, a coalyard, and a junkyard were not far away. We had black undertakers, doctors, dentists, bootblacks and hat blockers, seamstresses and photographers. There was a numbers house, a dance hall and movie houses. Bread and milk were delivered every morning and paid for at the end of the week. Vegetables, fruit, and fish were sold by street vendors, each announcing his arrival with a characteristic and often quite lyrical call. When we heard the shout "Fish here—I got your fresh fish here—25 cents, five pounds," I would dash out to make sure the man didn't leave until Clara had run to get Mom. My mother served fried fish with collard greens and cornbread, a menu that made my father say, "It's so good it'll make your tongue slap your brains out trying to wrap around it." Amen!

The ice truck came around in the cool of the morning, and each household had its own tongs for transferring a big block to the icebox. Once when I was a teenager we missed the truck, and I was sent to the icehouse. On the way back the twenty-five pound block slipped out of the tongs and landed on my foot, breaking my little toe. I carried the ice the rest of the way in agony. My toe set in a curled position, and Mom had the shoemaker create a pocket in my shoe to fit it. (I suffered pain and swelling for over thirty-five years—until finally in 1972 I had surgery to remove the bone. It left my toe looking like a shriveled little cocktail wiener left too long on a party tray. Long before that, though, when I was first married and still using an icebox, I used to get the shivering fits just looking at the tongs hanging in our kitchen. I thought I had died and gone to heaven when in 1949 my husband brought home a used electric refrigerator that kept the food cold and even made ice cubes!)

Garbage and trash were collected in separate trucks, after which water trucks wet the streets down and swept them clean with huge rolling brushes. We all took great pride in how our block looked. Every day we swept our pavements and scrubbed our white stone steps spotless.

For uninterrupted gas service, a meter in front of each house had to be fed a quarter every day. If money ran out between paychecks, Mom would try to cook up extra food before the gas went out. The street lamps ran on gas too, at city expense, and the lamplighter went around with his ladder at twilight.

Except for areas such as the row of handsome brownstones that housed wealthy whites on 18th Street south of Diamond, many neighborhoods were racially mixed. The races were cordial to each other but did not socialize. At the Liberty Theater (Broad and Columbia), they stood in the same ticket line, but once inside, whites sat downstairs while blacks climbed to seats in the balcony. The Bluebird and Uptown facing each other on Broad Street near Dauphin were all-white theaters, but when whites moved out of that neighborhood, the Uptown became a black-run business and hosted many celebrities. (It is closed now, but there is a movement to have it declared historically significant.)

North Philly's two black theaters, the Nixon Grand (Broad and Montgomery) and the Pearl (Ridge Avenue near 21st Street), had movies and stage shows featuring top-name big bands, dancers, singers, and comedians: Duke Ellington, Count Basie, Nat King Cole, and many more. I fondly remember paying eleven cents in 1938 to hear Chick Webb's band and watch Ella Fitzgerald—wearing a little girl dress, Mary Jane shoes, and white ankle socks—sing "A-Tisket, A-Tasket" as she searched the stage for her lost basket.

Early in our parents' marriage, the few times they went out together socially was to the Lincoln Theater on South Street. They thoroughly enjoyed such stars as Ethel Waters, Bert Williams, Bessie Smith, comedy team Bilo and Ashes, Ma Rainey, and the rest. But even though

Mom loved the shows, she was convinced that the people who performed in them were destined to go to Hell.

On Market Street was the beautiful Click Night Club. As teenagers, Clara and I desperately wanted to see Lionel Hampton there, so—we put on Mom's hats and stuffed our dresses in front and back. I'm sure the man at the door knew we were under age, but he let us in anyway. We ordered one ginger ale and took turns sipping it. What a show! Clara and I were always goggle-eyed and on the edge of our seats at any performance of the greats. How could we possibly have imagined we would some day share the same stage with many of them.

We sometimes went to South Philadelphia's black movie houses too, where the stage shows presented such stars as Fats Waller and Josephine Baker. The Lincoln Theater at Broad and Lombard broadcast a talent show each Sunday called *The Kiddie Hour,* and some of the children who performed there went on to sing and record well into adulthood. My mother took Clara and me to audition for the show, and they liked our voices but did not want us to sing the church songs Mom insisted on. She would not budge, and neither would they. That was the end of that.

Philadelphians love a parade, and the city is famous for its Thanksgiving Day Parade and the legendary Mummers whose New Year's Day extravaganza still brings flocks of visitors. Our parents would give Clara and me a dollar bill to spend on parade day. Mom never mastered money management, but outings like those taught Clara and me how to stretch a buck to the max. Our favorite was the Colored Elks' parade. Folks would arrive on North Broad early, with bags of snacks and jugs of lemonade, to claim "their" spots on the pavement. The party started with the first *boom, boom, boom* we could hear in the distance, and the cheering swelled up and down the parade route. When someone yelled, "Here she comes, I see her," there was no doubt who "she" was: Miss Flossie was high-stepping up Broad Street. Under an Elks parade cap worn half on her forehead and half on a shock of fuzzy red hair, her expression never changed: eyes looking straight ahead, lips bunched, chin up. Miss Flossie's arms swung in unison with those of the other

marchers, but from the waist down that gal was smokin'. Her ample butt
yanked at her short skirt with such intensity that her hemline vibrated
like gauze in a gale. Every year a man known only as Tall Percy moved
alongside the marchers, talking jive to her. And every year it was another show to watch the kids try to outdo one another steppin' like Miss
Flossie.

As the population of North Philly grew, so did the number of storefront churches. In addition to these and the larger established churches,
families and friends from "down home" often held Sunday services in
their living rooms, and traveling evangelists preached on random street
corners. And then there was Father Devine, born George Baker in
Georgia in 1882, who founded the Peace Mission Movement that eventually spanned the United States and beyond. Devotees—of all races—
gave all their worldly goods and assets to the Father, the "Prince of
Peace," who in return provided for their every need: food, shelter,
clothing, health care, work (everyone had to work), and spiritual guidance. Anyone, however, could get a really good meal at a Peace Mission
for fifteen cents, or even for nothing. Hungry folks had no trouble repeating the expected entrance mantra: "Peace, Father—it's truly wonderful." He was a force unlike any other of his time, and blacks admired
his financial and social (as well as religious) success. Mom used to say,
"If I ever get a church of my own, I will do what he had done—treat all
races the same by bringing them together as brothers and sisters." Many
years later, with Clara's help, she opened the Gertrude Ward Miracle
Temple for All People. Father Devine died in 1965, but the main mission is still located on North Broad at Ridge Avenue, and his widow still
lives with her "angels" in a palatial estate in Gladwyne, a suburban town-
ship.

Schools in North Philadelphia reflected the neighborhoods they
served: white, black, and mixed. Major studies were the same throughout, but the "extras" varied according to space and budget limitations.
We moved so many times that Clara and I attended ten different
schools. My interest in different kinds of music started in the elemen-
tary grades, where we were taught songs in the assembly room, and ex-

panded at Fitzsimon Junior High music classes, where we learned "Trees," "Danny Boy," "Beautiful Dreamer," "The Last Rose of Summer," and the like. It was as a soloist singing these songs in school assemblies that I first started holding the high notes—a precursor to what became known as "the high who."

*T*HROUGHOUT MY CHILDHOOD, each Sunday was spent in church. Our day began by attending Sunday School at 9:00 A.M. followed by the morning service. Next came BYPU (Baptist Young People's Union), and finally the evening service. The first Sunday of each month was Communion Day. This longer service took place in the afternoon. Mom would always pack a lunch, which we ate about halfway through our twelve hours in church.

The Ebenezer Baptist Church at 10th and Girard really rocked on Sundays. I remember a Pastor Childs, a snorting, rip-roaring devil chaser. Between him and the choir, I'm sure the foundation must have shifted many times.

The senior choir there evidently had, and exercised, the power of levitation: the sisters and brothers—to a head—could not keep their bottoms on the long wooden benches hidden behind the six-foot rostrum wall. The choirloft platform was elevated just enough so that when the singers did sit down, only their faces were visible. Clara and I used to call them the bodiless singing heads. We pretended that they had tiny feet under their chins.

In that church and others the whole congregation would change before our very eyes. As the service began, row after row held calm, sedate, well-dressed worshippers. The men all wore starched collars, ties, and jackets neatly buttoned. The ladies favored white gloves and fancy hats, cocked just so. But when the preacher had only just begun to speak, you could see signs of what was to come. There would be an "Amen" here and head-nodding there, or variously pitched voices crooning "Yes" and "Well." The paper fans (usually with an ad for the local undertaker on the back and a picture of Jesus on the front) would pick up speed. By the time the choir got really involved in one song or another, bodies in the pews would be jerking, skipping, clapping, fainting, shouting—just plain transformed by the spirit. Two things always amazed me: first, how some of those who had barely been able to hobble in to church now had some of the best and most vigorous steps; second, how the women kept their hats on.

Mom and Dad sang in the choir; so did Aunt Clara and Uncle Charlie. My father sang bass, Mom was a soprano, my uncle and aunt sang tenor and alto. People from all around said that Ebenezer had the best choir in the area.

Sitting up there in the choir loft my parents had an excellent view of the entire congregation—including Clara and me. During those long, long hours of attending services, we were not permitted to look at or talk to each other. If that rule was ever broken, we could expect and always received our lumps when we got home.

*W*E GOT lots of lumps in those days, but the first really vicious beating I remember was not for misbehaving in church. It was after Mom had given me two milk bottles to redeem for a penny each at the corner store and I made the mistake of trading one of the bottles for a jawbreaker. At six years of age, my judgment was less than logical when it came to goodies. My coming home with just one cent infuriated my mother, and she began to strike me over and over again—down to the floor, under the sink, into the kitchen furniture, everywhere. I could hardly catch my breath.

I remember sobbing and muttering, "Oh Lord, please don't let Mom go crazy and kill me." I had overheard my aunts and uncles discussing the nervous breakdown Mom had suffered some time before, and in my limited understanding of what it meant when people "go crazy," I thought my demise was imminent. I managed to get into a corner and curl into a ball, the same way we did when we rolled down a hill. The blows fell copiously on my arms and spine. When my head cleared, I was still in the corner but totally alone and extremely aware of the quiet and the scarlet welts throbbing their way up and down my body. I crept out of the kitchen, intending to get under my bed and hide, but Mom saw me pass the front room. She called out, "Willa! Willa! Come here." I thought I was in for it again, but to my amazement she sat me down at the foot of her chair and stroked my head. I was thoroughly confused.

THE REVEREND J. W. Brooks baptized Clara at five years old and me at eight. There was a play called *Heaven Bound* in which "the Devil" would try to entice the singers walking down the aisles. A few almost gave in but resisted. I was still too shy to sing so I just marched down the aisle, but Clara *strutted* down, just singing her little heart out: "Oh, when the Saints—go marching in—oh when the Saints go marching in—Lord, I want to be in that number—when the saints go marching in." That was her first solo. She was a natural; even at that early age her brilliance shone through. I was so proud of her.

But we didn't know where that brilliance would lead until shortly after Mom exchanged her work in domestic service for a job in a dry cleaning business. There, on a special day that was to mold the course of all the Wards' lives, an incredible and marvelously joyful event occurred: Gertrude's calling to sing Gospel. As she recounted it later:

I was pressing clothes in a cleaning and dye place at 19th and Mont-gomery Avenue in Philadelphia in 1931. As I stood there, I heard a voice that spoke to me so plain. It said, "Go sing my Gospel and help save dying and lost men and women." I answered saying, "Lord, I can't sing that good." The lady working at the next presser said, "Gert, who you talking to?" I told her what I'd heard. We both puzzled as to whether it could have really been the Lord.

I had always sung in the choirs and took the lead sometimes. But the Gospel? Hymns were one thing, but Gospel was another. Not long after that, I was invited to sing a solo at Ebenezer Baptist Church on Women's Day. It was the first time I'd ever sung alone, and I did "Since I gave to Jesus my poor broken heart, He never has left me alone. Since I for the homeland eternal did start, He never has left Me. . . ."

Later, standing on the corner of 40th and Girard Avenue with other dayworkers, I heard the same voice say, "Gertrude, sing My Gospel." The voice added, "Why look for a job when I've already given you one?" Well, I turned around, crossed the street, and used six of the eight cents I had for a trolley ride back home. With the other two cents I bought a few white potatoes. I boiled them and made some flour gravy, which we ate for dinner.

From that day on, I've had no other job but to sing for the Lord. A lot of them that have criticized me did all kinds of things to make money—but not me. Always singing for the Lord!

In the early days, Mom sang on programs with "belters" such as Janie Frances, Agnes DeShields, Roxy Williams, Sara Hinton, and Beatrice Green, each trying to wrench a stronger response from the audience. Mom was the only one with a soft voice, but when she got to humming and moaning in that mournful way of hers, there wasn't a dry eye in the church. It was as if God had put the new music in her soul; it came as naturally as singing all the other styles of church music.

A music historian has written that at first Gertrude Ward didn't un-derstand the music she was trying to sing, and that it was Thomas A. Dorsey who persuaded her to change her style to the new Gospel sound. This is erroneous; the truth of the matter is that Mom learned right along with the rest of those who were building on what Charles Albert Tindley and Lucie Campbell had laid down before (though she did say that Dorsey's solid, jazzy piano playing "beat the Gospel into folks"). Another lesson she learned from Tindley was to carry the message wherever there were people. Tindley, early on, sang at flophouses and pool halls and taverns, at spots where gamblers, prostitutes, and hustlers gathered—everywhere. Mom wasn't that radical in the beginning. It took her a long time to put the theory into full practice. From flatbed trucks to nightclubs was a long stretch, but eventually she did pull it off.

*I*N 1930, Mom had taken us to Anderson, South Carolina, to meet our relatives. Our grandmother Hannah had moved from the place in the country to town with her son, our Uncle David, who had a good job for the times: he was chef for a very wealthy family who adored him for his culinary expertise. The leftovers he brought home were precisely divided so we each had a like portion of his edible magic.

Our country cousins abounded. We met Anna Mae, Bill, Alvin, Johnny, Mae, Virginia, Seialah, and Nora. Then there were the uncles and aunts: Buddy, Foster, J.P., Ida, Floyd, William, Nathaniel, Idell, and more. It was a flourishing family tree.

While we were being impressed, Clara and I created a few impressions of our own. We really showed off singing our little songs and kicking up sand doing our "Philly steps." Two occurrences we hoped Grandma would forget. One was the time Clara and I started up Uncle Foster's car and changed the front end's appearance somewhat when it was stopped by a boulder that just sat there and didn't have the stone sense to move. The other was when we were caught under the bed with Grandma's pipe—but not before we had burned a hole in a prized quilt. Needless to say our butts were warmed for that one.

Mom and Clara went back to Philadelphia, leaving me in Anderson. I was more than glad to stay. When summer eased into fall, I went to live with my Aunt Mary and Uncle Arthur in the country. Those two were a study in opposites. She was soft-spoken, warm, and pleasant; he was stern. He didn't speak often, but when he did, there were no questions asked; his look spoke volumes. Fortunately, he was a reasonable and fair man.

Their daughter Uzeal, who lived nearby with her husband and darling baby, was a very loving mother. What Gerber did for baby food, she did country style: Little Mary ate what everyone else ate—after it had been dutifully masticated by her mom. I thought the practice quite distasteful, but Little Mary's healthy, plump little body was evidence that she thrived on this diet.

Since the local farmers hunted and fished, we all ate well on the game they brought back (rabbits, coons, ducks, pheasants, and fish) as well as the chickens and pigs raised at home. I got hysterical each time a chicken's neck was wrung and the body flopped over the ground, or a pig was axed in the head, but I recovered quickly when the cooking aroma came to get me. Once, when a traveling revivalist was invited to supper, Aunt Mary fried up three chickens and put the pieces on two platters; the one in front of the preacher's place held all three breasts and two drumsticks—until Uncle Arthur gave his wife one of his looks. When we sat down to eat, one chicken breast was on the platter in front of Uncle Arthur. That man's stare spoke as loud as if he'd used a megaphone.

I absolutely loved the farm life, the beautiful woodlands, and my new cousin playmates. Even picking cotton and doing other chores couldn't dampen my fervor. Our days were full, and in the evening, as in my mother's childhood, stories were told around the fire. The ones I enjoyed most were those of the supernatural. Almost everyone had seen balls of fiery light hanging or dancing crazily in the woods. When I came back north, I was told that what we had all witnessed was just swamp gas igniting, but folks from the country disregarded this silly, citified explanation. Then there were experiences with the "haint" that could take possession of you at night when you were horizontal. It would mount and temporarily paralyze your entire body except for the lips. You would try to call out but could utter no sound. Those who had been ridden by the haint told of their rapid heartbeat, of the heavy weight pressing them down, and sometimes of a long finger or fingernail penetrating the chest. When the visitation ended, you would be drenched in sweat but mobile and vocal again. Still other shivery stories were about animal responses to the unseen: horses, for instance, that would balk and refuse to move through a haunting mist slowly crossing the road ahead of them.

In the morning (when daylight had dispelled all the spooks), before going to school we collected eggs, fed the chickens, and eagerly anticipated Aunt Mary's scrumptious (she described anything really good as "scrumptious") breakfasts. That lady made heavenly biscuits that we saturated with homemade butter and dark, luscious syrup. The bacon would be thick, plentiful, and crisp. The eggs were minutes fresh, as was the new milk we spiked with three tablespoons each of coffee and brown sugar. You could almost feel yourself getting stronger with each mouthful.

My cousin Virginia and I enjoyed romping through the woods, swinging our lunch baskets as we frolicked, skipped, and laughed our way to the one-room schoolhouse six miles away. But I was amazed at the simplicity and shallowness of the teacher. I often knew the answers to questions she stumbled over, and I was skipped a grade after one week. Since the same teacher handled all six grades, though, what she didn't know for one level was added to what she lacked at the next.

When she saw how quickly I learned my lessons, Aunt Mary swore I was a genius, and she and Uncle Arthur decided to send me back to live with Grandma Hannah and Uncle David in town so that I could attend a Negro school that had teachers of higher caliber. They were usually women (with no such thing as forced retirement, a few of those old gals had taught my mother's brothers after they moved to town), and invariably they were married to the most influential men of the community. Another similarity they shared was light skin and straight or wavy hair. Surely these teachers were not inherently superior in intelligence to their rural counterparts; it must be that favoritism early in life, due to their appearance, had afforded them the benefits conducive to educational advancement.

The town school was much larger than the country one, of course; it even had reading books—one for every two students. We learned math from examples put on the blackboard by the teacher. But although it was better than the classes held in the Ebenezer Church, the school in Anderson was still not on a par with some city schools in Alabama, Georgia, and Florida, or with most northern institutions—as I learned to my sorrow when I returned to Philadelphia and was automatically put back a year, standard practice for southern students who transferred to northern schools.

I HAD been in South Carolina a little over a year when the time came for me to vacate paradise. Mom had sent a letter with my fare home and instructions for Aunt Mary to put me on the train heading north. Saying goodbye to the animals, secret nooks, and people I had come to love was one of the hardest things I have ever had to do.

Aunt Mary washed and ironed all the clothes I had brought from Philly that I hadn't outgrown and the ones she had so patiently sewed for me, and she cooked enough food for three people for my "lunch" to eat on the train. Aunt Mary, Virginia, and I sat on the lopsided bench marked "For Colored Only" at the end of the depot platform. We sat silently staring across the tracks into the distance where the treetops and sky smudged together. I remember Aunt Mary, her gaze still fixed straight ahead, grabbing my hand. I felt her love and sadness run up my arm and mainline to my rapidly breaking heart.

No longer in control, I flung myself into her arms as a wail tore from my throat. In an instant, Virginia, too was sobbing and begging me not to go. We were all still clinging together when the faint sound of the train's *click-a-dee-clack* eased into our consciousness, and a forlorn whistle announced the appearance of the steel-gray monster that was to gobble me up and end an era of joy I shall never forget.

I sat next to the window where Aunt Mary had placed my suitcase and the bag, almost as large, full of home-cooked goodies. The slowly moving train's frame soon eclipsed our anguished visual contact, but as it picked up speed each mile separating us tied the loving knot more tightly. I cried and ate my way into the North Philadelphia station.

I WAS feeling so sad and lonely that when I got off the train, Mom and Clara looked like angels to me. Clara was a little taller angel than I remembered, though still quite frail. I was really surprised when we went to 1300 Kerbaugh Street and Mom said, "Well, we're home." While I was down south, they had moved twice, and in a few weeks we were on the move again. The apartment I had come home to was barely large enough for two, so four people were two too many. This nomadic lifestyle was our lot during all the years I lived with my parents. Over a nineteen-year span, we knew twenty-four different rooms, apartments, and houses as home—returning to some of them more than once.

Our addresses included 1221 Melon, 1218 Harper, 1220 Harper, 2300 26th Street, 2224 Woodstock, 2257 Woodstock, 2000 North 21st Street, 2400 Dakota Street, 2200 Uber Street, 2222 North 20th Street, 2231 Lambert, 1800 Bouvier Street, 1517 Page Street, 1319 Fairmount Avenue, 3800 North 18th Street, and others. It seemed just as we got adjusted to new teachers, studies, surroundings, and friends, we had to move on and start the process all over again.

Our stay at most houses or apartments was stretched to the last hour before the landlord deposited our belongings on the sidewalk. Sometimes we left in the dark of night to avoid paying the back rent that my parents never seemed to have. Although my mother was a poor manager, my father allowed her to handle all household finances. The result was that even after combining his salary with her income (especially after she stopped working for wages in order to sing for freewill offerings), we stayed broke. I was often sent to various friends of Mom's to borrow money. Once, I remember I was dispatched to borrow fifteen cents' carefare from one woman in order to go borrow seventy-five cents from another, who worked as a domestic in Kensington—an area miles away from North Philly. Then I had to use fifteen cents of *that* loan to get back home. It took me two hours of waiting and riding time to bring home sixty cents—and to put us ninety cents in debt.

LTHOUGH WE never stayed anywhere for long, I have some very vivid memories of these various houses and the events that occurred when living in them. While staying on French Street, we went to "Camp Happy" for two weeks in the summer. It was located just across town in Northeast Philadelphia, but to us it was heaven. We swam, played games, sang camp songs around evening bonfires, saw movies, and were entertained by local artists and musicians. The camp directress—a Miss Dunn, whose mannerisms and appearance were very mannish—was a firm but fair person who kept the operation running smoothly.

We had to scrub and change our beds every day. Many of the kids wet theirs every night. The people who did the laundry surely must have had their fill of pissy sheets and blankets. One evening I was standing in the cabin looking out the window when a transparent white figure slowly passed. I wasn't one of the bed wetters, but I was just a drop short of saturating my undies when I saw what I saw.

After I related that experience, all the kids had a ghost story to tell.

Some said they too had seen spirits at the camp or knew someone who had. As scary as it was, we had great fun sharing these tales. Since I was on a roll, I told of a ghost that my cousin and I had seen on the second floor of her house. We were sitting on her bed talking about boys when we became aware of a shadow in the hall. Thinking her brother was eavesdropping, we ran to the door and saw a fat white man in a long, stained apron. He turned and went right through the wall. We were so shaken by the vision that we tumbled down the steps in a tangle of arms and legs, screaming all the way. The campers squealed with excitement as I recounted the tale.

Although Camp Happy was a summer camp for the poor, by no means did we consider ourselves anything less than privileged during the three summers we were able to go there.

In West Philadelphia there was an amusement park called Woodside. We always walked there from North Philly, saving our little bit of money to go on a ride and buy a hot dog or cotton candy. Most often we bought a box of that aromatic popcorn you could smell for a quarter-mile before reaching the park.

Clara and I knew every inch of that park—that is, all except the pool, the roller skating rink, and the area used for the talent show. "Colored people" were welcome to spend their money on all the amusement rides and concessions but were denied entrance to those three places. On especially hot days we would ride the ferris wheel (if we had ticket money). The operator would stop each car at the top for a short while, and from that vantage point we could see the white people frolicking in the sparkling water. How we longed to be in that pool also! We and other nonwhites had to cool off under a tree or with the aid of a flavored "snowball" that sold for a nickel.

We could use the city's public pools in North Philly, though, and that was one of our favorite things to do. My sister moved like a mermaid in the water. My swimming ability was just fair, but I loved it no less.

*I*N 1934, Mom decided to begin the tradition of annually celebrating her God-given gift of the Holy Spirit and
the ability to exalt it in song. This would be the first
of many anniversary programs and her daughters' introduction to performing in public. The illustrious guest artists she invited to perform
were Sallie Martin and Professor Thomas A. Dorsey. Wanting her first
anniversary to be extra special, Mom chose two of the best and most re-
spected composers and performers in religious music circles. Neither
had previously appeared in the Northeast, and they gladly accepted her
invitation.

Sallie Martin came on like a buzzsaw, cutting through a song with
jagged intonations that laid it wide open, rendering the meat of it raw,
and then—without changing gears—exuding a balm of absolute healing honesty. She knew how to "make ever-thang all rite," as she put it.
Her talented backup singer and pianist was a young woman named
Ruth Jones, who later achieved extraordinary acclaim as "Queen of the
Blues" Dinah Washington.

Thomas A. Dorsey spellbound the audience with his regal presence
and renditions of his own original material, including the popular "If
You See My Savior" and "Precious Lord, Take My Hand." Dorsey, often called "the father of modern Gospel music," had just struggled back
to prominence after having been shunned by church folk who thought
his blues influence unfitting—especially after he and Hudson Whit-
taker, as "Georgia Tom and Tampa Red," started recording risqué blues
in 1928. Mom, Sallie, and a few others remained friends and admirers,
however, until the other "Christians" caught up.

Mom's opening solo was "He's Never Left Me Alone," followed by
"Old Ship of Zion" and "Storm Is Passing Over." My solo was "Hide Me
in Thy Bosom"; Clara and I did "I'm Gonna Work until the Day Is Done"
as a duet; and Clara sang "When the Saints Go Marching In." Mutchmore Memorial Baptist Church was jammed with folks who gave up a

dollar per ticket; after the guest artists and the church were paid, however, there was just enough left for Mom to buy a clock the church needed and an ice cream cone *apiece* for Clara and me (usually, when we were fortunate enough to get even one, we shared it between us). Nevertheless, it was our true introduction into the world of professionalism—though all too often it was professionalism sans compensation.

May 30 was the date we chose to celebrate our anniversaries thereafter, although we missed it in some years because of commitments to sing elsewhere. Eventually, the Ward Singers became so well known that being asked to appear on our anniversary programs became a status symbol. Among those who participated—besides Professor Dorsey and Sallie Martin—were such legendary performers as Dinah Washington, Brother Joe May, the Reverend C. L. Franklin, Sammy Bryant, Earl Hines, Theodore Frye, Edna Gallman Cook, Clara Hudson, Rosetta Tharpe, Professor Earl Jones, Alex Bradford, James Cleveland, and Mahalia Jackson; and groups such as the Roberta Martin Singers, the Harmonizing Four, the CBS Trumpeters, the Soul Stirrers, the Gospel Harmonettes, the Dixie Hummingbirds, the Drinkard Singers (with Sissy Houston and Dionne Warwick), the Five Blind Boys, and the Swanne Quintet.

*S*OON AFTER my mother, my sister, and I started performing together, we were called the Consecrated Gospel Singers, and Mom would pursue any lead, widen any opening to get us on a program. I've seen pastors turn away when she approached them, hoping to dodge her silver tongue. Many, many engagements were agreed to just because it was hard to say no to that lady when she got warmed up. We got others by arriving uninvited at various churches early Sunday morning and offering to sing a selection at the day's service. If the offer was accepted, we'd fire the congregation up, hoping the teaser would result in a future engagement—and almost invariably it did.

Soon we were getting more and more invitations to sing, not only in Philadelphia but in Glassboro, Mullica Hill, Woodbury, Salem, Trenton, Lawnside, and other New Jersey towns. Sometimes the schedule was so tight that Mom arranged for us to sing at two different churches on the same night. On the weekends, the afternoons were also booked.

But something was wrong with Mom. Increasingly, she would become exhausted by the slightest activity; even singing a few songs wore her out. In the spring of 1935 she was diagnosed as having severe kidney stones, and then the kidney stopped functioning completely. She was in a hospital for poor blacks called Mercy Douglas, which was understaffed, underfinanced, and underequipped. The doctors there did all they could for Mom, but the prognosis was dire. She hovered between life and death for two weeks, while her weight dropped from 140 to 110 pounds. Then my father saved her life my moving her to Jefferson Hospital, where they removed the kidney and the threat of imminent death.

Daddy celebrated the positive turn of circumstances by purchasing brand new outfits for his girls and allowing us to travel to New York with our cousin Janet Burton, to see our cousin Maceo Hunter and Aunt Janet, who had moved there from South Carolina. Cousin Maceo treated us royally. We went to Coney Island and Radio City Music Hall without having to break the crisp one-dollar bills Daddy had given Clara and me to spend. It was our first trip to the Big Apple, and we had a wonderful time.

Clara returned with her dollar bill still folded. I came back with ninety-five cents—I had bought a pack of Wrigley's Juicy-Fruit gum to chew on the train. But two of the five sticks ended up in Clara's mouth to stop her pitiful and unrelenting begging.

HILE MOM WAS RECOVERING, we moved back to Aunt Clara and Uncle Hamlin's, where—thanks to their unselfish generosity—we stayed until a very, very ill Gertrude regained her health. They had replaced the player piano with a beautiful upright that graced a third of one wall in the living room. We got another opportunity to enjoy Cousin James's expanding musical ability. He would line up his six instruments next to the piano and commence cooking. All of us would sit mesmerized for hours to hear this fabulous artist slide, soar, glide, thump, pound, coerce, lull, coddle, and romance the melodies and magic out of each piece—wonderful!

But that was the good news. Clara and I always came home from school to eat lunch, and our cousin always seemed to be around when we did. One day as we sat munching our sandwiches, Acey (that's what we called James) came in and locked the door behind him. I sensed a difference in his manner, but at that time my lack of sophistication denied me the fear the following events would dictate.

Acey picked up his guitar, plucked a few notes, then announced, "We're going to play a game called Dropping the Panties. When I play these notes again, the first one whose panties hits her shoes will get a dollar." He plucked—but we didn't respond. Acey's face immediately rearranged itself so that all the lines were fractured and slanting downward. His eyes became evil messengers that warned us not to defy him. The game rules progressed rapidly as Acey proceeded to ravage my little sister and me. We moaned all through the incestuous violations and threats. He said our parents would be stabbed to death if we told anyone. The invasion of our innocence continued to happen at least once a week—even after we moved to a place of our own.

The end of it came when I told my mother and Aunt Clara. My first menstrual period frightened me more than Acey did; I was convinced I was having a baby. In the interim, Acey's girlfriend did get pregnant and

gave birth to a baby she named Marguerite. It's unclear when Acey
started to have sex with his daughter, but in time the trauma proved too
stressful for Marguerite, who escaped into a nervous breakdown and
was institutionalized for a time. She later recovered, bravely rejoined
the "peace of mind and spirit association," and often played the piano
for us in later years.

WHEN Mom's brother Arthur died while in the military, she came in for some of his insurance. The details were sketchy, but I clearly recall the benefits the money provided. We moved to a spacious third-floor apartment at 1908 North 18th Street, complete with brand-new furniture—including our very own Lester piano. We even got a break on the cost. The salesman put the decimal point in the wrong place on the receipt; instead of a balance reading $225.00, it read $22.50. (Our parents didn't correct the mistake.)

The movers decided (with good reason) against taking the piano up the staircase, which had three sharp, narrow turns. Upon deliberation, they decided the best and quickest method would be to hoist it up to the third-floor window. When we heard that bit of news, Clara and I ran out and gathered all available friends to witness the fantastic happening. We all sat lined up on the curb across the street, our eyes were glued on the huge object being hoisted skyward.

The men had removed the window and hooked up a pulley. When the piano reached the gaping hole in the third-floor wall, two men inside the room tried in vain to pull it through the opening. It was stuck. One of the movers from the ground floor went up to assess the situation, with all of us kids hot on his heels. He looked very much like a piano himself from behind.

We huddled in a corner trying to be unnoticed so we wouldn't be asked to leave the room. The Piano Man (or Man Piano) studied the problem and then, with a wave of a massive arm, signaled the other men away. Piano Man approached the jammed instrument slowly—legs wide apart, arms out, back hunched. Those mighty hands locked onto the straps around the piano and gave a mighty tug that succeeded in jarring it into the room by a foot or so. The "take charge" guy sucked in enough air to fill his lungs and grabbed the straps again. This time, man won over resistance and matter. The piano came crunching in, its momentum forcing the big fellow back and onto his knees. When he went down, he let out a yell and something else—soft popping and gurgling noises emerging from his pants. When Piano Man stood up, he was shaken and cursing like a sailor of old as a brown substance oozed down his boots. At that point, pandemonium broke loose. We were howling and rolling on the floor. Mom chased our friends out and made Clara and me go to the bedroom. After the movers had left, Ma tore us up— we cried and laughed through it all.

*I*N THAT apartment, for the first time I could remember, there was no food scrimping or dodging the landlord. There was even enough money to afford music lessons for me. My first piano instructor was a self-proclaimed "Professor of Music," Professor Burton, whose flamboyance taught me fluid hand and arm movements if not much else. My training was much more basic and practical under a Mr. Talifaro and Mrs. Estelle Carter and Edith Quinn.

Soon I was accompanying Mom on piano, and when I couldn't, Clara played for her—though Mom had to sing everything in F sharp because my sister still preferred the black keys. Even then, she showed a special quality and natural talent for Gospel music. Those tiny fingers stretched and maneuvered to work that F sharp to the max.

Eventually I taught Clara what I had learned and there was no stopping her after that. We both played for the Eureka Glee Chorus, which Mom had organized, and taught not only Gospel music but such difficult pieces as Rossini's "Inflammatus et Accentus," an anthem sung during Holy Week in musically discerning choirlofts the world over.

We both accompanied other groups and soloists as well. My first professional job of that sort, at fourteen, was with Anna Smallwood and the choir at Christian Hope Baptist Church, for which I was paid $1.50 a week. And when Mom supplemented her income by giving hour-long vocal lessons (at fifty cents an hour), I had the job of accompanying her students. Clara got a job playing for a Mr. McCrae, manager of a group called the North Carolina Junior Quartet. His daughter Ruth was their soloist, and Paul Owens, another member, went on to sing with the well-known gospel quartet called the Dixie Hummingbirds. Clara also played for the Reverend James C. Edwards, a fine Gospel singer who sang weekdays at several churches and broadcast radio concerts on Sunday nights from the New Central Baptist Church. This pace was almost more than my sister's frail body could endure. Often after a car ride home she had to be shaken awake from a nearly hypnotic slumber, or the Reverend Edwards would carry her into the house as she slept the sleep of a thoroughly exhausted child. By the time she was twelve, Clara was on the road playing for Mary Johnson Davis, traveling all through the Eastern Shore and on into the South, along with Bertha Wise and her wonderful male chorus. On all these outings, Mom was always on the scene as Clara's guardian, with me in tow.

Meanwhile, I was still practicing my popular songs; I knew every one that came out. To my father, though, any song that wasn't religious was "jazz." I had to say that it wasn't; it was a Gospel song. I had an opportunity to join a popular trio, but I knew I wouldn't be permitted to. It would be some years before my dreams of performing pop music would come true. I studied piano with jazz great James Weldon Lane later in my career.

*O*NCE my mother had recovered from the kidney operation, we returned to the grindstone singing at storefronts and churches. Mom also started managing the Taylor Brothers, young men whose talent was so raw and real it jarred your consciousness into elation. We were quite a package. The Taylors would whip up your spiritual appetite, then Mom's soft crooning would bathe your emotional palate in liquid soul. For the main course we served visual delights—two little girls and Mom rocking with the spirit—and our own brand of "Gospel stew," which seemed to fill the congregations' cravings.

It wasn't all success and kudos. One snowy evening, we walked eleven blocks to the Morris Brown Baptist Church located at 25th and Ridge Avenue. The snowdrifts were up to my waist, so Clara and I walked behind the Taylor boys, letting them open up a path with their bodies. When we got into the church, there was the preacher, the custodian, and six other people! After forty-five minutes no one else had showed up, so we sang to this small group. The eleven-block walk home found us collectively sixty cents richer—and frozen.

Even that episode could be considered successful, though, compared with some others—like the time we went all the way to Chester, Pennsylvania, in an ice storm, only to find the church locked up and no one on the scene to give us any information. We stopped about fifteen times to scrape the ice from the windows on the hazardous way home. Or the time we hired a man to drive us to Baltimore for a program. We rode around street after street, stopping and asking people if they knew where the Consecrated Gospel Singers were to appear. Mom had forgotten the name of the pastor *and* the church. We never did find the place. And since we had depended on the money from our appearance to pay the driver, he had a three-week wait for his few coins.

ORTUNATELY, AN occasional break in our strenuous schedule allowed for fun as well. In lieu of annual summer picnics, some churches and Elks lodges organized day trips to Atlantic City or Wildwood, New Jersey, and sometimes we were able to participate. The standard bus fare was five dollars for the round trip, leaving Philadelphia at seven or eight in the morning and starting back about seven in the evening. Once at the shore, the buses let us off in front of black-owned restaurants some three blocks from the "colored section" of the beach. The whites' beach ran the full expanse of the town's shoreline, with a sliver or two eked out of it for our use. No signs designated the borderlines between "us" and "them," but we all knew. If any of us did stray, a beach patrol officer would subtly herd us back where we belonged: "You lost, miss? I think that's the way you want to go. Your friends are probably over there."

The adults found this sort of thing humiliating, but we children were happy to be on the beach under any circumstances. And there were no such restrictions on the boardwalk or concessions; people stood in ticket lines and went on the rides in all unity and fairness.

I know of a few professional people who had the means to establish beachfront recreational areas that blacks could enjoy with pride intact. A Mr. and Mrs. Holmes once took Clara and me along with their daughter Anna and son Benjamin to a resort owned by Mrs. Janie Morris, a North Philadelphia funeral director who had bought a lovely, secluded tract of land on the New Jersey coast. She offered plots to her friends, who could build small houses there, and they and their guests could use the beach. It was not accessible to the general public, white or black, and the Morris Beachers guarded the location jealously, fearing that speculators would acquire surrounding property and eventually cause taxes to skyrocket out of reach of the folks who had created it all.

We heard this story from Mrs. Holmes as we cruised down the highway and then turned onto a branching road so small it seemed a mere stem—but a few bends of this stem took us to the blossoms, for there before us was a scene I had previously known only in the movies. Sparkling water danced over the sand; three pleasure boats rode at a small pier; five cabins were nestled in the pine trees. The Holmeses had not built their own cottage yet, but we were treated royally and had full access to all the food, swimming, boating, and good company this wonderful place had to offer.

Mrs. Holmes was a realtor who belonged to the Christian Science Church but had heard us sing at Enon Tabernacle Church in Germantown, two blocks from her home. She loved music, played the piano herself, and said she had been moved by our performance. Recognizing how exhausting our schedules were, this charitable woman afforded two young strangers a day in heaven. (Twenty-six years later I learned that my colleague Toni Rose had grown up in the Holmses' neighborhood and had known them well. It's amazing how life's dots connect.)

Another black-owned beach we knew of was on Amelia Island, north of Jacksonville, Florida. In 1935, Abraham Lincoln Lewis and Edward W. Watson, co-owners of the Afro-American Life Insurance Company, bought 200 acres of isolated shore property there as an area where blacks could live, vacation, and socialize without restriction. Eventually, there were private dwellings and motels, stores and restaurants, and many visiting celebrities to hobnob with. Today, however, American Beach finds itself in the situation that Mrs. Morris feared for Morris Beach: wealthy developers have acquired all the land on either side, and the 124 homeowners of this last relatively underdeveloped area of the island find themselves caught in a serious crunch. Perhaps the dream and the reality may be saved by current efforts to have American Beach declared a historic landmark.

*M*Y FATHER never protested our frequent moves or all the times Mom, Clara, and I were out singing. These things must have bothered him, though. There was little or no communication, but his outings with "the boys" became more frequent.

Daddy enjoyed a drink of whiskey every now and then, but Mom absolutely forbade any kind of alcohol in the house. One fateful day she discovered a pint of whiskey behind the couch where Daddy had stashed it, and holy hell broke loose. Our parents released all their pent-up hostilities and spewed angry words at each other. Usually Mom did all the fussing, but this time my father's tongue was equally acid and cutting. Eventually he threw his hands in the air, grabbed his coat and his bottle, and, in an instant, was gone.

Daddy was so unobtrusive, I hadn't thought about or really noticed him during the course of each day. But when he left and stayed away, the absence of his soft presence hit me hard. I still don't know where he spent the thirteen months he was gone from home. We never saw him except on Sundays—for Daddy never missed singing in the choir. Clara and I would look at him and then at Mom up in the choirloft, praising the Lord in song but not saying a word to each other when they came down. Daddy would nod to us on his way out of the church, but he didn't come over to us, and Mom wouldn't let us go to him either. Clara and I would squeeze our eyes tight, trying to wish and pray our parents together again.

The three of us went on singing or playing whenever we could, but without Daddy the money was less than adequate. It wasn't unusual for people to put a penny or nickel in the freewill offering—or to take the "free" part seriously and give the plate a mere glance. Consequently, it wasn't long before Mom deposited all our new furniture in storage and the three of us back in Aunt Clara's grace.

As benevolent as Uncle Hamlin and Aunt Clara had always been to us all, Mom resented the fact that they drank, smoked, and socialized with people she disapproved of. It must have been very difficult for her to live in that environment and not say anything, but I guess you don't bite the hand that feeds you or the hosts that shelter you. They had moved from the last house we shared with them to an even larger and nicer one. It was also out of the boundaries for those attending Harrison School, so we were transferred to Emerson.

WALKING to my new school one morning I heard a voice call out, "Hey girl, oh girl—come over here, I want to talk to you." I looked up to the window over Sal's Clothing Store and saw a red-headed woman beckoning frantically to me. By the time I had crossed the street, the woman was opening the apartment door next to the store's plate glass display window. In a few words she told me what she wanted and what she would pay. I ran home to ask if I could or should accept the woman's offer to take care of her two small boys after I left school each day. Needless to say, given our circumstances, Mom was all for it.

I started that job two days later. As soon as I got there, Mrs. Lumert gave me instructions and left. I was to keep the boys entertained until dinner time, then feed them, wash them, and put them to bed. I slept on the couch. Mrs. Lumert would reappear in the morning, and I'd trot on to school from there. Usually, I'd walk or run to school so I could use my weekly pay to buy the hot lunch, selling at twenty cents. If it rained, I rode public transportation; otherwise, I gave the remaining quarter to Mom.

Not until later did I learn that my employer wasn't going to work, as she had said, but playing house with her boyfriend. Mr. Lumert was a man with two jobs. He left home at 4:00 P.M., which is why his wife cautioned me never to come before 4:30. When I walked in, she was always ready to walk out, and I'd be gone before the unsuspecting husband returned to the apartment. Mrs. Lumert's boyfriend was a numbers banker known as "Goldie." I had seen him around the neighborhood many times but was not then aware of the connection.

One night the hockey hit the fan when Mr. Lumert came home between jobs to find his children in the care of a strange black girl. He asked me questions I could not answer about his wife. All I knew was, "She went to work." He left with his jaws "jammed with rocks" (poked out). About 6:00 A.M. he came back—to a still-wifeless apartment. He told me I could go, but I explained that when I left there, I went directly to school. I think it hit him then that this was routine and not just a one-night occurrence. Boy, did that man curse! When "Wifey" came bouncing in, she couldn't know that "Hubby" would soon be bouncing her from wall to wall. By the time I left, they were going at it hot and heavy. When I went back the next day, no one was there—end of job.

Every time I think of those two boys, though, I smile. Whenever I had to sing at a church program while they were in my care, I'd take them with me. They eventually got into rocking and clapping with everyone else. Whether they remember that or not, I'm sure something stirs in them—even now—when they hear Gospel singing.

*W*HEN MOM told Clara and me that Daddy was coming back to us, we hugged and cried for joy. It seemed strange to be that happy at the thought of being with him again—deliciously strange. The four of us moved to Uber Street together. Since money (or the lack of it) was still a problem, Mom started coaching singers and Daddy taught shape-note singing to a few people who were familiar with it. (In the South, many church choirs used this method; shape notes, representing the do-re-mi of the scale, are printed as geometric shapes rather than the traditional stems and ovals.)

After school let out for the summer, the three of us traveled more extensively than our usual three-state area (New Jersey, Pennsylvania, and Delaware); we took our act south. Although we had sung in the South whenever we went to visit family, this time we started out expressly for that purpose. We got off the bus in Virginia and were very grateful to be met by an elder of the church in which we were to sing. They were having a four-day tent revival beginning the next day. With the guest preachers, the church's choir, the testimonials, and us, we had a soul-stirring and -saving time. On the fifth day we left Lynchburg with warm hearts and loving spirits.

For the next few years we went to sing in rain, snow, wind, and heat—for handfuls or hundreds—on side roads, in open fields, tents, storefronts, quaint little churches, and impressive Baptist edifices. We sucked in pounds of road dust and gnats and hosted thousands of flies, man-eating mosquitoes, and bedbugs. We were often denied the most meager of food services and accommodations, chased away from well water, cheated by jack leg preachers, followed through towns by hate-spreading rednecks. We went hungry and thirsty, slept in depots and cars, stood on crowded trains. Sometimes we traveled for hours only to find closed churches or churches so cold we kept our gloves and coats on under our robes.

We also met some of the dearest people and experienced some of the most poignant, beautiful times of our lives. We were thrilled to be invited to sing at Tuskegee Institute in Alabama and even more delighted when the audience received us so favorably. (It was 1937 when Clara, Mom, and I performed there. Almost forty years later my group, the Willa Ward Singers, did a one-nighter there, and my two daughters—Rita and Charlotte—Sandra Peyton, Arlene Mills, Barry Currington, and I again experienced the warmth and excitement of a Tuskegee audience eager to show its love.)

At a high-class church in Atlanta we were a bit uneasy because the members seemed cool and quite reserved. Gussied up in a new look—leghorn straw hats and white suits—we opened with "Jericho Road" and then "If We Never Needed the Lord Before." At first we got a few amens, but with each chorus of each song the response got louder and less reserved. It wasn't long before the members of the congregation were jumping and shouting. After the program, some of the people said they hadn't reacted like that since the old days in their little country churches. We got so many compliments on our outfits that Mom decided to discard the traditional robes permanently. If it took different garb to grab the attention of those who were reluctant to hear Gospel sung—so be it.

*O*N ONE STINT, when we were to appear in twelve small Georgian towns in eighteen days, we had already done three programs and had a free day. Our next four days' stay just outside of Macon began with a warm greeting at the bus stop from a Sister Shannon. On the way to her home we got acquainted and exchanged pleasantries. Finally, the two-horse buggy stopped at a weathered but well-kept house, where we were shown to a small room with a bed made of split logs and a straw mattress. Clara and I were so tired we went to bed right away. The next morning we awoke to beautiful weather and a breakfast that was abundant and delicious. We helped with the farm chores and loved doing it. It was also a way to work off all that food.

The church was packed for the first program there. I never saw that many people get so happy so fast. It is difficult to explain that excitement and joy to one who has never been in that kind of environment and been moved by the spirit.

When we left the church, Deacon Shannon—our hostess's husband—was still happy. His booming bass voice punctured the darkness as he led us in his favorite songs, and the two horses seemed to trot in time as they pulled the full buggy homeward. We sat on the porch and drank tea until the relentless mosquitoes chased us indoors. The three of us retired to our little room and eased ourselves into bed and slumber. Until—"Get out of here! Damn you, Lucifer, get out!" I heard Mom shriek as the cobwebs cleared from my head. My eyes really popped when I saw a figure in white move toward the door. At first I thought it was a ghost—but then, a square patch in the white mass turned dark and I recognized the specter. Going out the door, in a pair of long drawers with the flap down, was Deacon Shannon's big black bottom.

Mom had us packed before morning. At first light, a silent, misty-eyed Sister Shannon hitched up the buggy for us and our belongings. I felt so sorry for her. As we found out later, the good Deacon had behaved in like fashion upon other occasions. His distressed wife longed to leave him but had nowhere else to go. No one uttered a word the entire trip to another church member's house about a mile and a half up the road. When we got there, Sister Shannon said something to our new hosts and was gone. We called thank-yous after her. She waved a hand but never turned around. I can't recall the other family's name, but they were quite gracious and made us a comfortable pallet on the parlor floor in front of the fireplace.

That Sunday afternoon we were shocked to see the Deacon in church, looking dignified and acting sanctimonious. We hadn't thought he'd have the nerve to show up. All the while we were singing, I kept sneaking glances at Clara and then at him. It was all we could do to keep from screaming with laughter. Clara's voice did break once, but she made it a part of her delivery and the congregation ate it up. Deacon Shannon sat on the bench in front of us, eyes closed, swaying in Christian rhythm, but all I could visualize was this pompous church officer as I had seen him the night before, with his fat drawerless ass exposed.

BY THE END of the eighteen days we were ready to go home; as it turned out, we came away with just enough money from the freewill offerings to take us there. We had insect bites that became infected. Clara's teeth and gums were a problem. So was Mom's intermittent diarrhea. Once home, we nursed ourselves as best we could. Daddy got some salve from the drugstore that seemed to help our insect bites heal, but Clara's mouth was getting worse. Finally she was taken to a dentist who diagnosed the ailment as pyorrhea.

Like Mom's family, most southern blacks had home remedies for nearly every ailment and a firm belief that with God's help the malady would heal or correct itself. Our family, too, tended to put off going to a doctor. In addition to the initial cost, there was the possibility of follow-up treatments that could strain our already inadequate household funds. As Mom grew older, she relied more and more on prayer as the solution to all problems. She often said, "Sometimes we think God has deserted us because His answer is not what we wanted it to be. Prayers are always answered. To our way of thinking, it can be for worse rather than better, but in the long run, it's always for a purpose that God chooses—praise the Lord!"

In this case, as well as I can remember, the dentist gave Clara some shots in her gums and instructed her to rinse her mouth three or four times a day with a mixture of baking soda, peroxide, and water. For a brief period her mouth felt better—which delayed the next dentist visit.

BEFORE WE SANG in Buffalo, New York, in 1935, we had never signed any papers or specified the number and titles of the songs to be performed. Whatever money we received was generally a portion of the freewill offering collected during the program. If the first collection was meager, the preacher or deacon would plead with the people to be more generous. "Now isn't this pitiful," he might say. "These young ladies done sang their hearts out, and they come all this way to give us a wonderful program. This bit of money is not enough to see them back home. Now don't embarrass your pastor— don't let them go back home and talk about us." This sort of psychology worked every time when the plate was sent around again.

But the preacher who heard us sing in Philadelphia and invited us to his church's revival in Buffalo sent us a proposal that stipulated a fixed payment for a specified number of songs (or more, if the spirit moved us). So this was our first contracted out-of-town job.

School was back in session, but Mom took us out for the trip. The day before we left, Clara had eleven teeth pulled, and on the train up to Buffalo she was still spitting blood. Mom kept praying to make it stop. She should have expanded her prayer to include pain eradication; poor Clara's bleeding stopped, but the pain persisted. She sang her heart out anyway. What maturity for an eleven-year-old.

This revival was scheduled for six days instead of the more usual four. We stayed at a house just a block away from the church. Mom and Clara shared a bed, but I got a small room and bed all to myself. It was dusk when we arrived at the house, and we had just an hour and a half before going to the church. After we got back, darkness and exhaustion made us totally oblivious to our surroundings, so when the bed I was sleeping in started to vibrate, I just assumed there were railroad tracks out back. There were about four "trains" that night. I didn't get much sleep.

As the lady of the house was preparing to take us food shopping the next morning, I mentioned the shaking bed. She stopped short. In a second she was sobbing out the story. There was no train. Her husband had died in that bed just four months earlier, and she had nursed him there for two years before his death. Afterward, she said, she had heard his cough and felt his presence many times upon entering the room.

Clara started to cry, "Don't let him get Willa, Mom, don't let him get Willa." That night I traded places with Mom, and Clara and I slept with our heads under the covers, praying that the man ghost wouldn't get our mother. There were no visitations during the rest of our stay. That must have been one ghost with good sense—you don't mess with Gert!

We decided to go see Niagara Falls on our last full day in Buffalo. We were so impressed we lost track of time and got back to the church too late for our final scheduled appearance. Our pay was docked for that evening. Still, by the end of the revival, I think more than half of Buffalo's black population had been touched by the Holy Spirit. Whether it was just for an evening or forever doesn't matter. If you receive the Holy Ghost even briefly, it is so glorious an experience you'll seek it again and again—until you cannot be without it and have been made whole.

ITH ALL our singing, at home and away, and all our moving from one address to another, our schoolwork had become harder and harder to complete. There were so many school changes, it was difficult to take hold of all the variations in teaching style and subject matter. You can't begin to imagine how delighted I was to learn, in spite of all the obstacles against it, that I would graduate from Claghorn Junior High School. I felt so elegant in the white organdy gown Mom made me for the ceremony. My music teacher put me on the program as a soloist. When I finished singing "The Last Rose of Summer," Mom came to the edge of the stage and handed me a beautiful bouquet of roses. (She always had an uncanny knack of creating instant impact.) Bobby Harris (who is now an excellent professional musician) played piano for me. We stood, hands clasped together, and bowed for the wildly applauding audience. That was the highlight of my life.

I was accepted into Girls High School, an academically excellent

Philadelphia facility, but I had to drop out after two years because of chronic tardiness and lack of homework preparation. Sadly, the same fate befell Clara after a year in Gratz High, even though the two of us tried to keep up with her homework assignments. All those programs and appearances, both weeknights and weekends, took their toll, and our chances for formal education were dashed forever.

O
UR ACTIVITIES were curtailed again when Mom developed a severe swelling in her neck that turned out to require a goiter operation. (That problem seemed to run in the family: four of us were afflicted with it—including me.) Luckily, our long-time friend Gladys Bonds and her husband were then staying at our house. They took care of Mom while the rest of us were at school or work, and I cooked when I got home. But Mom ignored the doctor's instructions not to speak for three weeks—much to everyone's regret—and that special Gertrude Ward sound was lost forever.

The one thing Clara and I didn't regret any time Mom was sick was the absence of our frequent beatings. There was one time, though, when my father saw a boy pulling Clara's arm and thought that was an act brought on by familiarity. We weren't supposed to notice boys. He started beating Clara with his belt. While my agile sister was ducking and dodging, Daddy missed his mark, causing his belt to whack him in the crotch. He let out a yell as he lunged for Clara, caught her dress with one hand, and tried to break his own fall with the other. The momentum his anger had generated sent them both through the vestibule door's plate glass. Miraculously, neither was cut.

When Mom got well, the constant singing began again. This time she had to change her style, but because our voices were getting more powerful, we could fill the gaps left by her injured vocal cords. Then a fine singer named Elizabeth Staples took Mom's place with our trio and proved to be a real asset. Thereafter, Clara, Elizabeth, and I took care of the singing, while Mom emceed and took up the collections. She would strut up and down those aisles working the audiences like a carnival barker. She could even extract nickels out of the stubborn penny-givers.

ITH ELIZABETH, we commenced another tour of the Southeast, chauffeured by a Philadelphia preacher who, I do believe, had a thing going with Mom. First stop: Wilmington, Delaware. Just outside of town we stopped for gas and drinking water. The proprietor readily sold us gas but refused to let us fill our gallon water jug from his pump. He apologetically but firmly informed us that the pump was strictly for his private use and not a part of customer services. He was kind enough to direct us to the "colored section," where we were fortunate enough to find more than water. The folks at the very first house had a well that we were welcome to use and a dwelling full of well-wishers. We gratefully accepted their hospitality, which included a scrumptious dinner and a good long rest.

That tour lasted all summer, but the preacher/chauffeur left us in St. Matthews, South Carolina, because his car was malfunctioning. We had barely been able to pay for gas, so a large repair bill was out of the question. We picked vegetables and did chores for three days as well as singing every night to save enough money for his trip home and payment for the farmer who agreed to take us to the next town.

And so it went for the entire season—hand-to-mouth feedings, hours of backboards and the backs of buses. Through it all, many afternoons and most nights found us happy and uplifted to be singing the praises of the Lord (but not too pleased with the platoons of southern bugs that seemed organized and determined to set up camp in our mouths).

Toward the first of August, Clara was complaining of fatigue and leg cramps. Whenever possible, Mom would put a blanket under a tree between performances to let her sleep and rebuild her strength. By the end of the month, we were all ready to stake out a resting tree. Although we had to stand for the first three hours on the train home, a ride to heaven in a padded chariot couldn't have been more divine.

*I*N MY teens, the closest I had come to dating was sitting on our front steps with a neighborhood boy. When the boy "accidentally" touched my arm or hand, I was thrilled to distraction but pretended not to notice.

I was kissed for the first time (not counting a few goodnight pecks) at my sixteenth birthday party. The older folks were having cake, coffee, and conversation in the kitchen while we were having a great time in the living room playing a game I had only heard of— "Post Office." In this game the "letter sender" stands in the vestibule with door closed and instructs the acting "postmaster" how many letters are to be delivered and to whom. Each letter represents a kiss. Example: four short letters and two long for Bob means that Bob joins the sender in the vestibule and gets four short kisses and two long ones. Bob then becomes the sender.

Everything was progressing wonderfully until Clara was called to receive letters. A minute later she came screaming out of the tiny entrance hall and bolted into the kitchen. In an instant the room was filled with Mom's voice and presence. She was raising the devil, and kids were falling over each other in their haste to exit. The party was over.

What had started out as a beautiful day ended with my entire back and butt covered with welts—all because a boy stuck his tongue in Clara's mouth. Somehow, Mom blamed me.

*M*Y FATHER was standing on the front steps when we arrived home after a three-month run in Richmond, Virginia. He looked a little sad, even though he was displaying his familiar "welcome home" smile. I so wanted to run up and hug him, but I dared not do anything so brazen. Instead, Clara and I yelled in unison, "Hi, Daddy."

As our parents exchanged the same words and the somewhat casual embrace that we had heard and seen on so many homecomings, I became aware of the young man sitting on the steps. After the hellos he eagerly offered to help with our luggage, and each time he took a bag in or came out for another, his smile and eyes were only for me. A rolling swell of most delicious and foreign emotion washed over my entire being.

Clara and I giggled and discussed the attentive new stranger till we fell asleep. I woke up several times, remembering his eyes and feeling that new something boiling inside me. The next morning, after Daddy had gone off to work and Mom had turned over for her second morning nap, Clara and I went scampering down the stairs to sit on the front steps. We were determined to catch the tall dark stranger coming or going.

About ten minutes had passed when we heard footsteps in the hall behind us. We almost got whiplash turning so fast—only to be disappointed by the sight of Mrs. Wilhelmina Washington, who lived in the first-floor apartment, leaving for work. But as she cleared the bottom step, she casually tossed over her shoulder, "Y'all met my brother John, didn't you? He's staying with us for a spell." So now the tall dark stranger had a name. John. *His name was John!*

In the next two weeks John Moultrie and I had more "accidental" encounters than you could count. Daddy must have sensed the vibes between us, because he spent a lot of time running John down and telling in great detail of the affair going on between him and the woman on the second floor. Nettie was middle-aged and not endowed with beauty, but my father was convinced that John was using her for her money and other "favors." Daddy might as well have been whistling "Dixie" for all the good it did to dissuade me from being totally enamored.

Mom proved how unpredictable she could be when she gave John permission to take me to the movies. We were soon dating regularly. One night he took me to the Congo Club on Ridge Avenue, which featured a shake dancer named Lila Mae Magee. I swear that woman shimmied and shook like jelly on a plate. I was absolutely amazed. John kept saying, "Close your mouth." I'm sure it and my eyes were full circles for the entire performance.

All the way home I kept wondering what it took to keep Lila's flesh and fringes vibrating the way they did. My account to Clara and our friend Dorothy, no matter how descriptive, never came close to what I had seen. I even tied the string part of a mop in front of my crotch and shook my middle until I was dizzy in the head. My captive audience was entertained and laughed a lot but couldn't possibly envision what my words and antics tried to convey. There was only one solution—they had to see that woman in the quivering flesh.

WE SET our plan in motion starting the very next day, frantically collecting and redeeming empty bottles, performing errands, saving the water-ice and potato-chip money doled out by our parents. The next Saturday evening found us at the threshold of the Ridge Avenue bar that showcased the talents of "Miss Lila Mae Magee—Queen of the Chocolate Shakes."

Five nervous minutes were spent on deciding who would enter the door first. We all had on our mothers' hats to give us that "older woman" look. My borrowed disguise with the heavy black veil and tall crown

got me elected as the one to break the smoke barrier of this totally un-
familiar adult atmosphere. The doorman gave us an arched brow and
knowing grin but let us in. We found our way through the semidarkness
to a table against the wall near the back. Shortly, a five-by-five waitress
brought us the pitcher of beer and three glasses we had ordered for a
quarter. We poured the brew into our glasses and laid our cigarette
butts in the ashtrays (we had collected the longer cigarette stubs from
the trolley stop and put them into an empty cigarette box discovered in
the street). And then, we waited.

Dorothy kept giggling, and we kept poking her sides. After getting
this far into our adventure and this close to the viewing, we didn't in-
tend to draw attention that might result in our being put out. The band
was jumping and so were our pulses. By the time the blues singer had
socked out a few blistering tunes, we were chomping at the bit. Then—
finally—after being introduced by the saxophone player, the phenom-
enon known professionally as "the Queen of the Chocolate Shakes"
(but to the man at the next table as "the Twirlingest Butt in Philly") siz-
zled onto the stage.

Lila Mae did the quiver—the roll—the trimble—the single bump—
the double bump—and bumps unknown to common man. She worked
on her knees—her back—all fours—one leg—and just plain flat-footed.
Lord, that lady could move! At the end of the performance we sat there
mesmerized. We were soon jarred out of our trance by an irate waitress
who demanded our departure. It seems she was convinced that one of
us had urinated on the floor. Actually, the puddle that ran from under
our table, nearly causing her to slip, was the beer we had tossed on the
tiles instead of down our throats. Nevertheless, we had to leave—but
no matter; our mission had been accomplished.

The fun I had anticipated of reviewing the night's events on the way
home—wasn't. Poor Clara was so embarrassed by the waitress's accusa-
tion that she wailed the whole distance, punctuating her noisy sorrow
with "I hate bars," "I can't stand that nasty dancer," "That storytelling
waitress is the meanest ol' thing alive." She swore never to enter a bar
again.

The fear that Clara might tell our parents about our outing kept me petrified for the longest time. Thankfully, that fear was never realized, but after our bar adventure she seemed to have changed a bit. Though I couldn't put my finger on the difference, it was enough to stir in my guts. I still had a loving sister, but a part of my play buddy was missing.

ONCE AGAIN we were on our way to Mom's old home in South Carolina, and this time Daddy made the trip with Mom and Clara and me. Aunt Mary met us at the Anderson station, sitting in the familiar old wagon we had come to know by its peculiar tilt and every creak and squeak. We were instantly bathed in the warmth of what must have been the most beautiful smile in all the South (even with the tooth missing on the side).

That evening we had a singing, eating good time. New stories were swapped and old ones retold (with a little yeast thrown in to keep them activated). My father was the star; he sang as we had never heard him sing before. His soul was definitely showing. His curling smile reflected his pleasure at the unanimous praise showered on him. But the next evening, you would not have known the face that met us in the yard as the same one. The serenity and gentleness had fled, leaving the countenance stony hard and the soft smile completely upside down.

The reason? Earlier in the day we had been given permission to go with our girl cousins into the woods to search for "kudos" (turtles). But the girls had another plan which, we agreed, was far more exciting than the original. About half a mile up the road, two boys in a car were waiting for us. We eagerly climbed in and were on our way to visit the Civilian Conservation Corps camp outside of Anderson. (CCC camps had been established by Franklin Delano Roosevelt's administration to create work for America's young men who could not find it elsewhere. Although they were segregated, blacks and whites both took advantage of the program and were glad to do so.) We howled and hooted all the way there. It was also great fun talking with the guys at the camp and eating the candy bars they offered us. On the way home the boys gave us a grand tour of the countryside and various farms before taking us back to where we had met.

We knew we were in trouble when the setting sun found us still a mile or so from the house. It was dark when we got back. Our entrance into the yard was met by "Here they are—here they are—thank God. Oh Thank God!" Everyone was shouting praises, questions, or words of anger. My father took it further; he started beating me with a branch he snapped from a tree. Being afraid that some harm had befallen us made Pop crazy. He whipped me so long and hard that my mother intervened for the first time in her life.

When I gathered my senses, I realized the yard was full of strangers, including the sheriff and two of his men, neighbors, and many relatives. Someone had seen us get into the car with the boys and had told Uncle Foster and our parents. The agonized worry that set in was further developed by passing time. Our folks started thinking about abduction, rape, or murder. When deep concern turned into panic, the sheriff was notified.

The situation cooled a bit after we told and retold the activities of our day. All but the live-ins left and went their separate ways. But when our group had been reduced to just immediate family, the fire of anger was rekindled, and once again the heat was on. Uncle Foster began switch-whipping our cousins, while Mom exercised her arm on Clara and me, and everyone was vocal in some way—yelling, pleading, crying, or cursing. It must have looked like a madcap movie fight scene with the big people winning.

That night we kids compared our welts and decided we would all run away from home. The ham cooking for next morning's breakfast replaced our hurt with hunger, and by the time we were washed and dressed, our only thoughts were on what other goodies would accompany the ham. After eating, however, my mind snapped back to the question of escape. I'd had it with the humiliation and hurt of being whipped. John was the solution. I would marry John.

*J*OHN HAD BEGUN driving us to our local engagements whenever his tired, beat-up car was in operating order. He was doing odd jobs, so his time was flexible.

He had resigned himself to the idea I had persistently embraced that I would "save myself" for marriage. Imagine his total surprise and delight when I not only came on to him and stimulated his libido but acquiesced in its ultimate fulfillment. My plan to make my parents receptive to my marriage really worked, for I was soon pregnant. When Mom found out, John was terrified; I was overjoyed; my parents were furious and insisted on a quick wedding. The year was 1940.

I chuckled inwardly all the way to the altar. My new husband was twenty-one—I was nineteen. We moved to the third-floor apartment in the house where John's sister, Annie Mae Frazier, lived. Mom, Pop, and Clara moved to an apartment on Susquehanna Avenue over a Chinese laundry.

I continued to sing with the group throughout eight months of my pregnancy and resumed when my baby was just seven months old. I wanted to stay home and fulfill my role as mother and wife, but John persuaded me to go on singing and traveling. He would say, "That's your mother. You can't let her down!"

*B*ABY CHARLOTTE'S first tour with us was down along the eastern seaboard. Elizabeth Staples was not with us. We started in Maryland, and then went on to beautiful Williamsburg, Virginia, where they were refurbishing the stately old structures and upgrading the colonial aspects of the town. Unfortunately, the improvements stopped short of the black sections. A really lovely family opened their home to us—as rickety as it was. All four of us slept in the same bed with me lying crosswise at the foot.

Luckily, the first night there, I had decided to put my baby to bed in my open suitcase on the floor; otherwise, she might have wound up, as we did, covered with lumps. We had no idea we'd be the main course at the bedbug banquet. Clara jokingly said, "I'm gonna put just my legs in bed so I'll have big legs when I wake up."

When black folks rode buses down south in those days, the designated seating was in the rear section. When we got on, we had to start at the very back and then take seats in front of that until we filled it to the rear doors. More people than seats meant that standing up was the rule. If many white people boarded, blacks had to give up whatever seats were needed.

The plus of bus travel was lower cost and periodic chances to stretch our legs at the comfort stops. We always got more exercise than the whites because we had to walk around back to get served—if there was time—or run to the woods to relieve ourselves rather than use an overflowing, smelly, filthy toilet. This and a long traveling time were among the minuses.

Trains too could present problems, as we discovered in leaving Virginia for a booking in Clemson, South Carolina. When we heard our train being announced, we gathered up all our bags and my baby Charlotte and headed for the very front of the train where "colored" could enter (the white people got on conveniently near the depot door). Clara dropped a suitcase, which popped open when it hit the platform. We quickly scrambled to recover the spilled contents and started running for the front of the train—past the dining car, the sleeping cars, and the white coaches. We were nearly there when the train started its ever-quickening roll southward. A conductor standing in the doorway waved "bye-bye" as his laughter first angered, then outdistanced us while we stood there with our mouths open. We had no choice but to spend the night on the colored benches, wrapped in clothing from our suitcases to keep the night chill at bay.

The next morning we made sure we were in the right spot ahead of time. For some reason, there were a lot of colored people heading south that day. With only two cars allotted to us, we were really crunched in. Children and women sat on the seats and suitcases in the aisles; even the toilet served as a resting place between more serious uses. Men stood wherever there was room and relieved themselves in some leakproof container on the connecting boarding platforms. Whichever guy brought the level to the top had the job of emptying the collected liquid along the rushing countryside. I've had better journeys.

We had left Philadelphia before July Fourth; Labor Day found us in Blue Field, West Virginia—broke. John and my father had to send us the money to come home. We enjoyed being home for two months— then it was back to Virginia again. In Roanoke we got a room at the colored hotel, which had very reasonable rates. We quickly developed the habit of sitting on the huge windowsill opposite the front desk. This was the favorite gathering place for hotel personnel, guests, and anyone passing who wanted to socialize.

On December 7, 1941, we were chatting like magpies with the radio sounding in the background when the person behind the desk shrieked, "Oh no! Pearl Harbor has been bombed!" It took a couple of hours of constant listening for the horrible facts to sink in. Everyone was terrified. We wondered if and when the States would be bombed. We had a prayer meeting right there in that small lobby. Then we hurried back to Philadelphia to be with our loved ones on familiar ground.

C LARA'S SINGING and playing abilities rapidly gained in intensity and complexity throughout her girlhood, aided by the ten-inch, 78-RPM records of the era, which we played on a hand-cranked Victrola phonograph. Two of her singing idols were Queen C. Anderson and Clara Hudson, known as the "Georgia Peach." The piano playing of blind Arizono Francis, who recorded as early as

1936 for the Golden Gate label, was full and pulsatingly vital. It served to reinforce and fine-tune Clara's development of a like style that was hers from the beginning.

Once we were well enough known to attract "name" performers to join us, we always enjoyed it when any of these "idols" stopped in for a visit. A few hummed notes would invariably develop into hours of spiritual fusion, or a casual mention of "back home" would initiate endless stories of the past—with a few southern style jokes thrown in for good measure.

Clara Hudson dropped by whenever she was in the area. My sister and I loved the way she dominated a chair. She always sat at a slight angle with her big dark body obscuring the entire seat back (Clara and I never failed to imitate her after she left). Sometimes her husband would come with her. He was a preacher named T. T. Goldson. The couple had a habit of folding their hands in their laps the very same way. The Reverend would sit with his eyes closed, rocking gently from side to side—chuckling or adding something to his wife's tales about the "old days." We especially liked to hear her tell of the romps and escapades she and Tom Dorsey had as youths in Atlanta, Georgia. Those were the days preceding their inevitable titles of "Georgia Peach" and "Georgia Tom" or "Professor Dorsey." Clara H. said they were both "out there," but T.D. didn't let anything pass him by. Her huge frame shook with mirth as she recalled those earlier times.

When she had an anniversary program in New York, we were her guests. The young girls in her group—youngsters from an orphanage school in Georgia—complemented her own magnificence, bringing raw energy and purity to the seasoned Georgia Peach's program. The mix was exciting. The girls were ecstatic at being in the "far North" and also enjoyed the accolades showered on them. Their mentor led the praise and clucked over them like a mother hen. Clara and I acted cool, but we too were excited about being featured singers at the legendary Savoy Ballroom. (Years later, we were honored to have Clara H. appear on one of our anniversary concerts at Philadelphia's Convention Hall.)

Dinah Washington, whom we had known since she was Ruth Jones, was another visitor. Dinah's first big record was with Lionel Hampton doing "Blow Top Blues." She knocked folks' socks off with her absolute earthiness and a voice that could instill the blues into your very core.

One spring when the cherry blossoms were in full evidence in Washington, D.C., we were working a five-day church revival and Dinah was at the Howard Theatre with Lionel Hampton's band. On our first day in town, Dinah came by to invite us to come hear her that night. She had a long fur boa that she carelessly tossed on the bed. Her eye brows were plucked and her nails were long and red. She seemed so exciting and worldly. We were fascinated with the stories she told of her wild adventures on the road. Then, when every eye was glued on our friend as she stood on the Howard's stage, I imagined myself there in the spotlight, singing my heart out. The feeling was delicious. I would have traded places in an instant.

It was quite evident, when I saw Dinah twenty years later in Atlantic City, that she had gotten off the world at the wrong stop. I went up to her with a fond "Hello" and hug—only to be dismissed with an uncoordinated wave, a glassy stare, and a slurred, "Give your name and address to my secretary." She obviously had no idea who I was. Ruth Jones was far removed, and Dinah Washington was fast losing it. I walked away, sadly aware that we both had lost a good relationship. I thought—"I'll miss you, Ruth."

Rosetta Tharpe's effervescence permeated our home regularly. On one occasion, she and dancer Bill Bailey showed up at our house at the same time. Bubbly Rosetta started humming and clapping in stop time, creating a rhythmic platform for Bill to build on. He started tapping one foot, then the other, and was soon totally engrossed in a full-fledged performance. Daddy, Clara, and I were clapping time and adding our own gleeful encouragement to Bill's stepping. I guess Mom thought we were enjoying the show too much. "That's enough, that's enough," she yelled—ending the joyous soiree.

Rosetta, or "Li'l Sis" as her intimates called her, from the days when she sang with her evangelist mother, Katie Bell Nubin, was getting acclaim—and some disapproval, because she was recording secular numbers with Cab Calloway and Lucky Millinder as well as religious music.

She felt, as did Professor Thomas Dorsey, that all music was God's creation and therefore couldn't and shouldn't be considered sinful. Some Christian folk disagreed. Not that Rosetta needed anything other than her natural buoyancy to keep her "up." Her hit record "That's All" was being bought by huge segments of the "colored" population nationally. Her Memphis-styled guitar playing was chock-full of blues chords, which she rolled together masterfully with her voice.

The Baileys were the only family not criticized for mixing W. C. Handy's music and Negro spirituals in the same breath. Pearl Bailey's path to stardom began humbly enough when she won an amateur contest at the Pearl Theatre on Ridge Avenue in Philly. Little did she or anyone else know that her rendition of "Poor Butterfly" would launch a career that transcended race, time, and space. Many thought Eura Bailey sang better than her sister, but fate fell differently for her; decades of nightclub singing brought Eura only modest success. Brother Bill, when performing on stage, would interject biblical passages or condemnations with his routine. Needless to say, audiences cooled and became less receptive to his remarkable tapping artistry. The bookings became sparse and then nonexistent.

Shortly after that, Bill heard and heeded the call to preach the Gospel. His first big sermon was delivered in New York City at the famous Savoy Ballroom. We were invited and went to hear it and sing with him. The hall was crowded with friends, well-wishers, and family, including his sisters Vergie, Eura, and Pearl. Unfortunately, Bill was the only one inspired. The sermon (I'm sure it was sincere) lacked fire in context or delivery. Small wonder he drifted off to other pursuits. The last time I saw him, my (second) husband and I were passing 15th and Pine Streets where he was working as a doorman. Bill asked us to lend him five dollars. He said Pearl was due in town and had promised him some money—we'd be paid back from that. A short time later some hoods from the neighborhood beat him severely. I was told he never really fully recovered. Poor Bill! I'm sure God would not have endowed him with such marvelous dancing talent if He had not wanted him to use it. What a waste!

FTER JOHN and I were married, Clara was con-
stantly at our apartment trying desperately to soak
up as much togetherness and connubial bliss as possible—secondhand. When I was holding Charlotte or sharing a tender
moment with my husband, I would often see tears glisten in my sister's
eyes. She told me later that she was afraid the war would spread over
here and take her life before she ever really lived. Before long her spo-
radic tearing developed into full-scale sobbing sessions. In the middle
of one she shouted, "I'm gonna do the same thing you did; I'm getting
married—I'm getting married as soon as I can."

Of the assorted fellows sniffing around Clara, the obvious choice
was the one who sniffed longest and with the most gusto. Clara was sure
Richard Bowman would gladly reinforce all that heavy breathing with a
marriage contract, and sure enough, one day she came rushing in to de-
clare, "We're gonna do it—we're getting married." She was so eager to
be liberated and loved that she was convinced marriage would insulate
her from all harm and provide constant happiness. The main thing she
hoped for was a cutting of the chains that bound her to our mother's
domination.

Elkton, Maryland, was where all the area folks went to be married
when secrecy or urgency made elopement necessary. Two weeks after
deciding on this course of action, we found ourselves third in line for the
jiffy marriage ceremony we had driven to Elkton to participate in. From
the string of signs that read "Justice of the Peace" or "Unite Here," we had
chosen the place that was least crowded. When their turn came, Richard
and Clara stood before a boxlike structure covered with white linen. John
and I stood in back of them as their witnesses. The man behind the box
nodded to the short, fat woman at the organ, who began playing softly
"Oh Promise Me." As the last note of the first chorus vibrated to a slow
ending, the man said, "I now pronounce you man and wife."

On the way home, Clara and I sat in the back seat of the car, giggling, crying, exchanging sentiments and saturated handkerchiefs. Clara was not as worried as I about telling Mom of the wedding. She had already taken courage from being Mrs. Bowman and was almost eager to confront our parents, whereas I would just as soon have gone to hell in a pair of gasoline drawers as face Mom with such news.

Mercifully, John took over: as soon as we all were inside, he blurted out, "Well, say hi to your new son-in-law." All hell broke loose. Mom's mouth was agape for just a second, then filled with shouts and curses directed at me. "You're the cause of this. Clara wouldn't have done this if you hadn't encouraged it. Damn you! You're only good for having babies; now you want Clara to be the same. I'll break your neck if you don't get the hell out of here now." She took a swing at me which my husband blocked. My father held her back as we four made a speedy exit.

The newlyweds got an apartment on Diamond Street, near our parents. I'd never seen Clara happier than when she was cleaning, decorating, cooking meals, and the rest of it—she really loved saying, "my husband." Daddy came by to see if he could help in any way with the apartment and to wish Richard and Clara the best. Mom wasn't speaking to any of us.

We enjoyed the silent treatment for a week. But soon Mom went to see Clara and Richard with a totally civil attitude. We concluded that she had realized just how much everything she was building rested on us. It became evident, though, that she considered me a threat, and from that time on she systematically worked to separate me from Clara. Richard was also on the hit list. When we were home, Mom practically camped at the Bowman apartment. Instead of Clara having more freedom, Richard was slowly but surely losing his. They were subject to interference and demands at every turn. Mom was driving them crazy— but then, that was the plan.

After two and a half months of marriage, the Bowmans began a new addition to the family. Clara experienced difficulty from the beginning, yet Mom seemed to accelerate the frequency and number of programs. There were times when Clara had to leave the platform to throw up in a coffee can she kept close by at all times. Someone else would take the lead until she came back to sing, and I would slide onto the piano stool and pick up the accompaniment where she left off.

Because of the war, more money was available to the working class, which meant we got better pay for our appearances—even if it still came from freewill offerings—and it wasn't a struggle to get to the next town anymore. We went to Newark to do five performances in three days. The three evening programs ran about three and one-half hours each; the two afternoon programs were two hours long. The pace was exhausting for all of us, as usual, but it really took its toll on Clara. She was extremely tired and so ill that when we arrived in Philadelphia, she couldn't make the short distance from Mom's apartment to hers. Later, Elaine Pesta who lived in the same building, told me she had had to pick Clara up off the floor and put her on the couch. My sister begged her not to tell my mother.

Just six weeks after Newark, while we were having chorus rehearsal at our parents' place, Clara had to go to the bathroom. She had been complaining of stomach cramps, which she thought were caused by drinking too much ice water. When she hadn't come back after a reasonable time, I went to see if she was okay. She was sitting on the toilet moaning softly and drenched in sweat. I ran to get Mom. Shortly thereafter, the hopes of there being a third member of the Bowman household were flushed down the toilet. That was the closest Clara ever came to motherhood. My sister's hurt and sorrow cut into my heart like a saber.

The Bowmans celebrated their first anniversary with a big dinner party at their apartment. Besides the family, the guests were members of the Roberta Martin Singers—Bessie and Paul Folk, Norsalus McKissick, Eugene Smith—and many other friends. But the anniversary repast turned out to be a "last supper" for Richard and Clara. They had an argument that evening which Mom got into. "You should not have gotten married in the first place—following that Willa," she yelled. "God put you here for bigger things. You're being punished." Clara went home with Mom and Daddy that night, never to return to Richard. They were quickly divorced. At eighteen and a half, she was once again a forlorn little girl named Clara Ward.

*I*N 1943 we were invited to sing at the National Baptist Convention in Chicago. Each year it is held in a different city, and this was the first we had ever attended. Being selected to perform was most exciting. All the singers and music had to be approved by the Baptist "high priestess," Lucie Campbell, the most influential woman in the largest black organization world wide. After the first full day of the convention, Baptist folks from all over the country set up workshops, lectures, and booths displaying promotional materials, pictures, records, and sheet music for sale. Throughout the week, the evenings were heated with sermons by hordes of preachers. The preaching and singing that went on during that convention touched the very core of even some religious pretenders (those that fake their faith).

There were so many singing groups on the opening night's program that most were limited to one song. We did four. Of them all, every word and note of Thomas A. Dorsey's "If We Never Needed the Lord Before" captivated singers and listeners alike in the joy of the Holy Spirit. Clara put her whole heart into it, while I hit and held those high notes, which came out sounding like "whooooo." I was the one who started that feature, now called the "high who."

Our friend Mahalia Jackson had a beauty shop on Chicago's South Side at that time, and she styled our hair beautifully. Her technique of pressing and "croconoling" (deep-waving) was absolutely the best we had seen anywhere. Those hairdos lasted three times longer that when anyone else did them. When we asked how she did it, her eyes crinkled almost closed as she flashed that gorgeous smile of hers: "It's my secret, self-developed pomade and these magic fingers." Those magic fingers could also whip up a fantastic Creole gumbo, which we thoroughly enjoyed at her house. We couldn't stay for the entire convention, but while we were there, she kept our hair deep-waved to the max and our stomachs filled with excellent cuisine.

Mahalia had branched out from singing in churches to working larger and more financially rewarding venues. She titillated Mom's interest by urging her to get a white manager who, she said, would have better connections and could get more money for bookings than black managers, no matter how good they were.

CLARA AND I were invited to several parties after the first night's program. We didn't know till later why Mom was not asked; at the time, we told her we were going to eat with some of the younger people and then go look around town. The first party we hit was in the same hotel where we were staying. Two adjoining rooms on the next floor up, were stocked for either a huge mob or a long- and hard-partying few. We helped ourselves to some delicious food and sat down on the bed to enjoy it, but soon the odor of burning marijuana took our appetites away. We got out of there in a hurry.

A few days later, two gay fellows took us to a party at the home of one of the others in their singing group. Boy, that was a revelation! Three of the preachers who had inspired the people to holy dancing and shouting were now doing their own inspired thing—with other men. As dark as it was, you couldn't miss the activity going on in the two bedrooms, the doors left open for easy access or turn-on.

Downstairs, folks were eating, dancing, drinking, telling jokes, enjoying themselves. But of about thirty people there were only seven women, and the other five were obviously lesbians. We had met plenty of gays and usually had great fun in their company—it was easy to admire their creativity and wit—but I couldn't for the life of me understand why Clara and I had been invited to such a party.

I soon got my explanation when one of the young men we had come with bounced down the stairs in a T-shirt and a towel, on his way to get some ice. In passing he excused himself for not entertaining us but offered, "Honey, I'm on a mission. When Mother gets back upstairs, she's gonna dive right in the middle of all that flesh. Clara, if I'd have thought about it, I could have invited someone for you. I know this sharp young child who'd just love you, she's a Stone man, Honey." The guy probably thought I knew, but until then, I had no idea that my sister had dabbled in homosexual activities. She was really embarrassed that I had heard, and we were both so uncomfortable that we left.

Neither of us had brought any money for a cab, however, so we sat on the steps and talked until our friends came out—about three and a half hours later. Clara revealed that she had engaged in a clandestine affair with someone we had worked with. Mom had imposed upon her an abstinence and loneliness that was intolerable. She was vulnerable and open to anything that filled that void in her life.

I asked Clara to tell me about "liking girls." She said, "There's not a lot to tell. When you get real close just close your eyes tight and put your mind on somebody you really like a lot. Willa, you know my thing is men, but Mom gets between me and any man I decide to get tight with." I prodded my sister to tell me more, but she kept drifting off to other subjects. Never again did we approach that topic, and never again did I ask her about her involvement with lesbianism.

Mom evidently got wind of the party activities, though, for she began ranting and raving about infidels and disguised devils infiltrating the convention. Mom did fiery mini-sermons about sin and corruption wherever there was a captive audience. She believed that the mix of lambs and wolves was the same for those who attended worship services and those who did not and felt she had to take up the banner for the devout and faithful Christian majority.

UNT CLARA had kept Charlotte for us during the convention—as usual, she was there for the asking—and I was six months pregnant with my second child. My sister would put her hand on my stomach and sigh wistfully or murmur, more to herself than me, "I wonder what my baby would be like."

Clara and I had lost that little-girl closeness, but we still shared a tight bond, and my new awareness of her emptiness prompted me to include her in every family activity that might fill some of that hunger in her. When my second little girl was born, I asked Clara to name her. She chose the name Rita Claire.

John and I had by then rented a house on Thompson Street. It was in terrible shape, but my husband's decorating and carpentry skills soon transformed it into an attractive, comfortable home. Then, just as we were really enjoying our little castle, John was drafted into the army and stationed in Dothan, Alabama. With my husband gone, I concentrated on my daughters and singing. Our group had expanded to include singers Catherine Thompson (of the North Philadelphia Juniors), Ruth Johnson, Marie Millsap, and pianist Gladys Gordon.

Aunt Clara kept my children when we traveled to Winston-Salem, North Carolina, for eight full weeks of programs. At the Teachers College there we had a contest with a wonderful group from the area called The Camp Meeting Choir. Each group put up one singer of the same voice range (alto against alto, soprano against soprano) for judging. As good as they were—we won. Some years later, in Detroit we entered a similar contest against the Meditations, Della Reese and her sisters. Della was singing high then. Her voice was absolutely beautiful, and those girls really showed off. That night the cup was theirs—deservedly so.

The Thompson Street house John and I had refurbished was obviously done too well. The owner put it up for sale without telling us—she must have shown it while I was away singing—and gave me a month to vacate. John suggested asking my parents to let the children and me stay with them until he could come home and make other arrangements. We were crowded but managed until Mom and Daddy purchased a house (their first) on North 18th Street. I gave them the money John was sending me to help out. The down payment came from an appreciation program that was given for Mom's efforts to further the success of Gospel music and singers. A bushel basket of money was presented to her, which amounted to $360.

More and more we were expanding our horizons. No longer were our services restricted to Baptist churches. Sometimes we were asked to sing in churches whose worship format was subtle and contained. No matter—our programs were tailored to suit all. I always sang Negro spirituals and songs such as "Trees," "Nobody Knows the Trouble I've Seen," and "Danny Boy." After four or five numbers of that sort, we would test the water with a little spritz of Gospel. Invariably, after easing them into the spirit, you would be hard pressed to distinguish those folks from a down-home congregation.

Whenever I would move the people with a solo, though, Mom would give that song to someone else to perform. She said, "You're trying to outsing Clara. You'll never do it. She is the one people come to hear." It had never entered my head to try to top anyone. I was only trying to do my best, which I thought would be best for the group as well. But even Clara was showing signs of Mom's influence. When I played for her solos, which had suited her just fine until then, she would sometimes stop singing and roll her eyes at me. One time she even came over to the piano and made me get up so she could finish the song playing for herself. I was totally embarrassed but sang my background harmony just as if nothing had happened.

Sometimes I wouldn't know about a concert until it was time to leave. Gladys Gordon or David Riddick would go along to play so Clara could stand up and front the group. Mom would say to me, "You need to stay home with the children and keep your father company."

*T*HANK GOD for us all—the war ended. John came home from the army in one piece, and we resumed our beautiful life together.

About that time a preacher and Mom worked out a deal where she would negotiate with a local radio station that played Gospel to broadcast our engagements from the various churches. The arrangement was for a fifty-fifty division of the ticket money with the church and a fifty-fifty split of the money put out for the advertisement. Some of the preachers didn't honor the deal, keeping all or a major portion of the money, and not one of them split the advertising cost. They really did Mom a favor. Her disenchantment with them prompted her to do it all herself, and so "Madam Gertrude Ward, Promoter" came into being.

Mom was soon booking soloists, duets, trios, quartets, and full choirs, and sometimes preachers and evangelists. Our own group was on the move. People would stop us on the street and ask, "Aren't you a Ward Singer" or, "I was really inspired by your singing—where are you going to be next?" Tickets were sold for some programs, but the majority of them were still compensated by freewill offerings.

Our group was ever expanding and changing, adding and releasing people to meet the immediate need and circumstance (I've put full lists in the Appendix to this book). One major addition came when Mom booked a program at a Holiness church in West Philadelphia, and a Leola Cosby called to ask if it would be all right to add an aspiring soloist from Florida to the program. Mom was a little reluctant to accept an unknown but acquiesced after Mrs. Cosby promised that she would never be sorry. As it turned out, that was the understatement of the millennium. When the time came, a short, plump girl took the stage, opened her mouth—and brought the house down. She sang with unbelievable versatility, command, and spirit. This girl was the great Marion Williams. When she, Henrietta Waddy, Mom, Clara, and I hooked up, we were awesome!

Our cousin Marguerite Shaw, daughter of the musical James "Acey" Burton, also played for us from time to time. She played really well and accompanied the Ward Singers in performances all over the country, and the Gertrude Ward Singers when they toured Japan. We were sorry to lose her when she fell ill, but time and professional help eased her back to health. Thereafter, when personal problems began to weigh on her, Mom would let Marguerite work and travel with the group, hoping the change of atmosphere would lighten her load. Thus, she played for us off and on for twenty years, until she was incapacitated by a stroke in 1967. She is currently in a nursing home.

Throughout the late 1940s the Ward Singers were spreading Christian joy nationwide and in Cuba and Canada too. Sometimes I toured with them, sometimes not.

*T*HE YEAR of our biggest anniversary celebration was 1949. Tindley Temple is a huge Philadelphia church, but there were so many people crushing to get in that we hurriedly decided to do two programs, back to back. The folks lined up around the next corner from the church stood waiting for two and half hours—seemingly just glad to get a chance to hear us. John and his brother David Moultrie and my father were on the doors. The money was coming in so fast, they had to use trash bags. All together, over 10,000 people turned out.

The next two nights we appeared in Washington, D.C., at the Uline Arena. The Reverend Robert Cherry's National Gospel Foundation, Inc., sponsored the concert, featuring Edna Gallmon Cook and the Ward Singers. Everyone was stunned to find that we had drawn 14,000 people—and you must remember that this was without the massive advertising campaigns of today. No other Gospel singers, then or now, ever drew such crowds. After the second night Marion Williams said,

"I'll be able to put a down payment on a house." I don't know if the other singers received the same amount as I, but if they did—$150 would not a down payment make. I was so disgusted.

Luckily, John had become known as a fair and good handyman and had made money enough to purchase our first house, on Smedley Street.

T WAS a milestone year for the Wards in other ways as well. One afternoon I was upstairs folding sheets when I heard the sharp, insistent sound of a car horn. I finally looked out the window and saw a fabulous vehicle that seemed longer then my house was wide. Imagine my shock to see Mom sitting in the front passenger seat and Clara behind the wheel. I didn't even know she could drive, and here she was in a brand new $7,500 fishtailed green Cadillac. They had paid cash for it. No wonder the rest of us received so little money for the Tindley Temple and Uline concerts.

Eager to put "the Hog" on the road, Mom arranged a tour to California. John offered to drive so he and I could be together. We had a stop in Chicago, where our performance went very well. Mahalia, as did everyone, simply adored the Caddy.

In Oklahoma City we finally found a place that allowed us to spend the night—the first motel I had ever stayed in. The proprietor was Mexican and had probably run into a few obstacles himself as a nonwhite. The rising sun found us on the road again. We were behind schedule, so John kept his foot on the pedal except for gas stops. He surely earned the $50 a week he was paid to get us where we had to go.

By the time we arrived in Las Vegas, we were all plagued by hunger. We had hoped to quell our pangs and move on—no such luck. Unexpectedly, conditions were just as bad here as in the South—maybe worse, for in the South, we could at least get served at the back door or window of restaurants. In Vegas, wherever we stopped, we were directed to a place in the "Negro section."

After bumping over trenches and dirt roads, we found the "greasy spoon" disguised as a luncheonette. Under normal circumstances we would have sped by this dreadful place, but our growling guts influenced us to buy the dry, tired pressed ham sandwiches they sold. A gourmet lunch it was not. As bad as the food was, though, we were later glad we had eaten it, because we couldn't even get a bag of potato chips in Bakersfield, California.

That year, the Baptist National Convention was held in Los Angeles, and San Francisco was hosting the Elks Convention. We had a singing good time in those two cities—but all for freewill offerings. It was a bit unsettling to travel such distances and have no inkling how much money we could depend on, if any. And again there were times when after driving half a day or more, we would get to a church only to find it totally dark and locked up tight.

On the up side, though, the Reverend E. T. Lewis, pastor of Mutchmore Memorial Baptist Church in Philadelphia, and been invited to preach at a huge, prestigious church in Los Angeles, and when he learned we were in the area, he asked us to participate in the Sunday morning service with him. The church elders didn't like the idea; "Gospel singers are too loud," they said. They felt we lacked the sophistication their congregation was accustomed to, but they backed down when Pastor Lewis threatened to cancel his appearance.

The morning of the service found us a little nervous but ready. We opened with "Jesus Is All the World to Me," which I had arranged. Clara, Marion, and I blasted the line "When I'm sad, He makes me glad, He's my friend." Then we dropped the volume. Marion and I did a spot obbligato in high register and close harmony with Clara ad-libbing. We could see listeners twitch in their seats— we knew their reserve was crumbling. By the time we eased into our heavy hitters, the congregation was crying, shouting, and holy dancing in the aisles. Even the ushers lost control and joined the joyous happening. Pastor Lewis came to the pulpit facing folks who had been drained emotionally. I think he had wanted us to warm them up, not use them up.

After that our programs were packed. Selling books and pictures afterward raised enough money to send John back east and pay another driver from Philadelphia to meet us in California. Our bills were mounting at home, so John had to go back to get some of the debts paid. The whole tour lasted three months.

ANTING to get in as much action as possible while we were in California, we were guests on the Dinah Shore show, Martha Tilton's radio show, and Hattie McDaniel's *Beulah* show. Later, at Hattie's house, we met Eddie Anderson (Jack Benny's "Rochester") and his brother.

Hattie talked extensively about her Black brethren. "We all like a basket of crabs—content to lay there clicking as long as no other one moves. Then as soon as one tries to climb to the top, they all start to climb by pulling the top one back and stepping on him. They pull off a leg or two if they are in the way."

She was upset by her negative mail from blacks condemning her for accepting roles as a domestic, such as her Oscar-winning part in *Gone with the Wind*. "They mad at me cause I'm too fat, black, and countrified, and Lena Horne for being too yella, glamorous, and citified. Instead of them being glad that we finally opening the door for others to come, they just want to close the door till Jesus step through. Any progress is better than going downwards. We are our own worst enemy. You would think they'd be writing us letters of praise for breaking through, and buying the products our programs endorse, but no—they want the show canceled. Lord, when we gonna learn?"

Mom chimed in, "You right, Hattie, we're taking the Gospel over the country like it never has been before, but the little-minded don't want to share the Lord with sinners. If not with them, who need him most, then who with?"

There were "amens" all around the room. That brought on a lot of ethnic "inside jokes." Everybody had at least two, and Eddie Anderson and his brother "swapped lies" till our bodies were aching from laughter.

We all performed, too, and I sang a popular song that fascinated Eddie. He asked me to send him a dub of me doing standards, but my husband squashed the idea when I got back home. (A "dub" is a demonstration recording made in a small studio with a minimum of performers; for example, a singer will be accompanied just by a piano or other single instrument. It is not meant to be a professional product in itself. Its sole purpose is to introduce an artist or a song to record companies for their consideration. In Chicago we had made some dub records where Mahalia had hers done, but at that time no one was interested.)

O N OUR WAY home from California we had a concert in El Paso, Texas. And since Mexico ranked high on the list of places we wanted to see, we decided to visit Juarez the next day. At the border the officers warned us not to take the Caddy into Mexico; they said, "If you drive in, there's a strong possibility you all will be hiking back. The pirates will take it from you." We did as they suggested—left the car stateside. Unfortunately, years of expectations of what the exotic country would be like dissipated in the steamy 109-degree temperature as we trudged from one vending stand to another, purchasing souvenirs to commemorate a day best forgotten. We brought back twenty post cards, three straw fans, and a load of disillusionment. The most exciting thing about that excursion was Clara's fainting in the suffocating heat. But things were soon looking up again for the Ward Singers . . .

Gertrude and George Ward, with Clara (in George's arms) and
Willa (standing), 1925. *All photos from the author's collection.*

Gertrude Ward (left) and daughters (Clara, Willa), 1937.

David Murphy, Gertrude Ward's father, 1917.

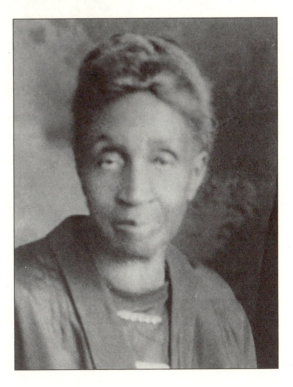

Hannah Murphy, Gertrude Ward's mother, 1917.

Arthur Murphy, Gertrude's brother, and (inset) Irene Murphy, her
sister, 1918.

Clara and her husband, Richard Bowman, 1941.

Dinah Washington on a visit to the Wards in Philadelphia, 1941.

Dinner party, Washington, D.C., 1942. Sallie Martin is seated fourth from the left; Gertrude, Clara, and Willa are at the far right. The inset is a photo of the hostess, name now unknown.

The Ward Singers on a tour of the South, 1942. Left to right: Bernice Davis (at piano), Gertrude Ward, Elizabeth Staples, Clara Ward, Luellen Price, Willa Ward.

Hattie McDaniel, star of the *Beulah* show, with Gertrude Ward, Hollywood, 1949.

The Ward Singers' first photo after the release of "Surely God Is Able," the first million-seller Gospel record, 1950. Left to right: bottom, Gertrude Ward and Clara Ward; top, Henrietta Waddy, Marion Williams, Willa Ward. *Photo by Michael Denning.*

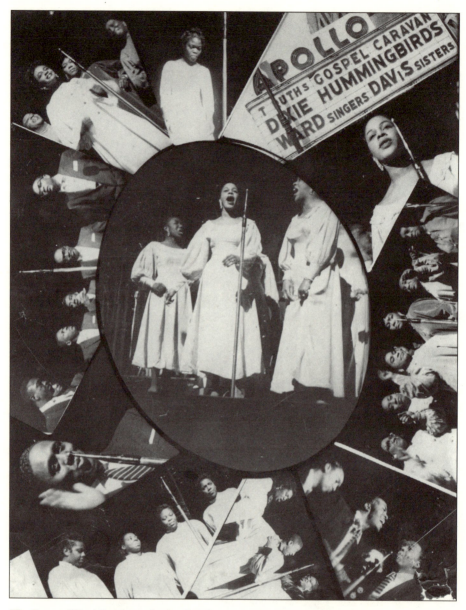

The Famous Ward Singers at the Apollo Theater, 1952. Center: Willa Ward.

Clara Ward Specials, 1952. Left to right: bottom, Frances Johnson, Lillie Davis; top, Frances Steadman, Thelma Jackson.

The Ward Singers entering through the audience at Philadelphia Convention Hall, 1951. First to last: Gertrude Ward, Marguerite Shaw, Marion Williams, Willa Ward, Henrietta Waddy. Twenty

thousand people attended this performance. *Photo by G. Marshall Wilson.*

The Famous Ward Singers with
the trophy presented by the
Pittsburgh Courier to the "Best
Singers of Gospel in America,"
1953. Left to right: Marguerite
Shaw, Thelma Jackson,
Henrietta Waddy, Willa Ward,
Gertrude Ward (holding
trophy), Marion Williams,
Frances Steadman, Clara Ward.
Photo by [Walter] Mosley.

Clara in her purple, twelve-
passenger 1957 Chrysler
limousine. *Photo by Wert S.
Hooper.*

Willa Ward (right) and
Lionel Hampton (center)
backstage at a concert
in Detroit, 1955.

Willa with her husband John Moultrie, after winning a hat contest at Philadelphia's Met, 1955.

The Famous Ward Singers at the
Newport Jazz Festival, 1957. Left to
right: Kitty Parham, Gertrude Ward,
Willa Ward, Clara Ward, Marion
Williams, Frances Steadman. *Photo by
James J. Kriegsmann.*

James Burton and Aunt Clara, Gertrude's nephew
and sister, 1957.

Part Two : 1949–1963

ON THE SWING back east we had an engagement in Knoxville, Tennessee, sharing the stage with the Gospel Harmonettes. In their program they sang one of Clara's favorite songs, William Herbert Brewster's "Our God Is Able." She had often heard it and sung it herself, but somehow this time it made a real impact on her psyche and played constantly in her head. We could hear her humming or singing it all through the day. She finally announced, "I'm going to record it as 'Surely God Is Able' in an entirely new arrangement that no one has ever done."

My sister played the melody over and over again, trying different tempos and rhythms, her body swaying with the unusual patterns her fingers were pulling from the keys. Finally, eyes closed as she played, Clara said softly, "This is it—we'll do it in three-quarter time." Triple time, of course, has been used for many kinds of music, but it was rare in Gospel, and for that brief, inspired, creative moment we felt that it was ours alone. As Clara played the melody and we got more and more into the "call and response"—"Surely . . . " "*Surely* . . . "—our excitement mounted. We worked and worked on the arrangement until it was indelibly burned into our minds and we were ready to rehearse it with the whole group. Clara would begin: "Surely, surely, he's able to carry you through . . . " and then the others would sing the first verse, "As Pilgrims here we sometimes journey . . ." while I held the high note. Then Clara would sing, "He was Moses' bush burning, . . . Joshua's mighty battle ax," and so on, until Marion came steaming in with the last verse: "Oh don't you know God is able . . ."

We had been under contract to the Savoy Recording Company for several years, and our frustration and disappointments were almost as old. The first series of our songs pressed by the company were very good but had not been enthusiastically pushed. In fact, religious recordings in general lagged behind secular ones, and our platters had been left to simmer on the back burner. Now, when we let the Savoy people hear our rendition of "Surely God Is Able," they raved over it—yet they dragged on with excuse after excuse for their delay in recording it.

We felt so strongly about our arrangement of the song that we just couldn't let it lie. Clara suggested taking it to another company, and we chose Gotham, with whom we'd had some previous dealings. Gotham, as excited about "Surely" as we were, waxed it and saw an immediate response. People were buying the record all over the country, and headlines lauded Gertrude Ward, Clara Ward, Willa Ward, Marion Williams, and Henrietta Waddy, who had made a million-selling record. Individual artists had recorded million-sellers, but the Ward Singers were the first Gospel group to do that—much to our delight, even though we got only $125 for recording the song. We had been so anxious to have our arrangement pressed that we might even have taken less!

When Savoy, which still held our contract realized that the Gospel hit sweeping the country was ours, it sued Gotham to get "Surely" back. By then, however, the market was saturated.

THROUGH THE years, many folks have credited Marion Williams with singing the entire lead on that record. Another legend has it that Brewster had approached Marion to propose that she record the song. The facts, however, are otherwise, and this may be the time to dispel a number of inaccuracies that have been passed on to the public by reporters and music historians.

First, Brewster had no knowledge of our recording "Surely God Is Able" until he, like everyone else, heard it on the radio. When he did, he called Clara to tell her how much he loved it and also suggested that they work together on other songs. That's how their collaboration came about when Ward's House of Music opened three years later. We were the major publisher for Brewster's music, though he was also published on a smaller scale by the Bowles Music House in Chicago.

Second, it's been said that Brewster discovered Clara and provided her first break by letting her sing during the intermission of one of his plays. This did not happen. By now readers should have some idea of what Mom was like; no way would she have allowed Clara to be "discovered" without all three of us being discovered.

Third, it was rumored that Clara pirated the song "How I Got Over" from Brewster. Not so. Clara reworked an old spiritual we sang as children into the hit rendition we recorded; she had it copyrighted in 1951.

Fourth, one paper published a "Spotlight on Clara Ward, Gospel Soul Queen" that is easy to ridicule. The piece called her a tall, dignified woman (she was five-feet-two). It said she had a daughter who died in a house fire at age six or seven (Clara had no children). It credited hers as the first Gospel group to work at Radio City Music Hall, in 1963 (that was the Willa Ward Singers—Clara never performed there). It said she appeared in the movie *It's Your Thing* (the film was *A Time to Sing*). It declared that she sang with "faith healer Reverend Leroy Jenkins, which she did, but identified him as pastor of the Church of 'What's Happening Now'" (that was comedian Flip Wilson's "church" on his television show).

Another reporter once wrote that "Clara Ward worked on the dock as a stevedore before hitting it big as a gospel singer" (at a whopping ninety-eight pounds? Sure she did!). But enough already—back to the truth. Clara and the Reverend W. H. Brewster worked well together. By the time Ward's House of Music closed in 1965, they had collaborated on many songs that became staples in the Gospel repertoire. Brewster was such a remarkable and prolific composer that many major Gospel singers eagerly performed his songs: Sam Cooke and the Soul Stirrers, Alex Bradford, Mahalia Jackson, Rosetta Tharpe, James Cleveland, Queen C. Anderson, and of course the Ward Singers. Not only was his music as good as it gets, but he wrote the first two Gospel songs to become million-selling records: "Move on up a Little Higher" (Mahalia Jackson, Apollo 164), and "Surely God Is Able" (Clara Ward and the Ward Singers, Savoy 4017).

*B*EFORE we did the record, we celebrated our homecoming from California with a program at Philadelphia's elegant Metropolitan Opera House. Again thousands were denied entrance to a hall already filled to capacity. The program lineup, headed by our dear friend Mahalia Jackson, included also the Reverend C. L. Franklin, Professor J. Earle Hines, Brother Joe May, the Reverend B. J. Small and Mary Johnson Davis Small, and midget evangelist Sammy Bryant.

Mahalia had sung with us at the Met earlier on a program promoted by Celestine Jennings. Celestine was a protégé of Mom's who was often put in full charge of the singers when Mom was busy elsewhere. Clara and Mom had taught her how to put all aspects of a complete program together, and Mom suggested that she produce a show featuring the great Mahalia Jackson and the Ward Singers for her first test run. That night was graduation for Celestine: it was a total success.

We had first met C. L. Franklin in Detroit after he entered the ministry, and our paths had often crossed since then. This time, however, the Reverend and Clara seemed to share the Holy Spirit intermingled with the human spirit. It was the start of my sister's one and only heart, soul, and flesh real romance.

*O*UR SCHEDULE remained hectic, at home and on the road. In the middle of one tour, Mom lost her appetite and was so thoroughly exhausted that she made the sensible decision to go home and recuperate. The rest of us continued on to Richmond, Virginia, where we ran into a terrible storm. We finally found and checked into the "colored" hotel, hurriedly changed our clothes, and went to the church hosting our concert. We stood there bewildered and drenched looking at a carelessly written sign that read "Singing Canceled." We sloshed our way back to the hotel after stopping to purchase a box of saltines and two cans of tomato soup. Yet as disappointed and broke as we were, that night held more fun and freedom that we'd ever had traveling the road with Mom. We sang, told jokes, and played cards using torn newspaper as thousand-dollar bills. The man on the desk lent us the cards and offered to sell us a bottle of corn liquor, which we declined. Upon our return, Mom couldn't understand why we weren't disturbed about our bad trip.

CHILDREN'S DAY in the South is a highly celebrated festivity. We liked singing at these celebrations because of the joyous fellowship—as well as the rows of tables laden with deliciously cooked soul food: ham, chicken, pepper sausage, boiled pork, meat pies, headcheese, fruits, vegetables, pies, rolls, biscuits, cakes, and more.

During the day the program is handled by young people, who come to the church sparkling like new coins from head to toe. Even shoes and clothes that have seen much service are scrubbed, pressed, and polished to look their very best. These programs always open the same way. A tiny girl, hands on hips, recites this poem:

> What you looking at me for?
> I didn't come here to stay.
> I just came to tell you
> That today is Children's Day.

Then each child offers a song or a reading, and some present short skits. By late afternoon, eyes will be rolling toward the door that leads to the anticipated goodies. In the evening after the feast, adults sing songs for, preach about, and praise the children.

Once when we were happily on our way to sing in Atlanta for such an occasion, we stopped at the first service station off the main highway in Georgia, intending to gas up. A man sitting on a bench outside the wooden office building jumped up and yelled through the screen door, "Hey, you all, come on out here and look at these niggers and what they riding. Hoo-ee! You all gotta see this."

Three other men popped out of the doorway and started excitedly exclaiming to each other about our Cadillac—how large, how roomy, and how pretty it was. Then one of them said to Mom, who had gotten out to stretch her legs, "What you doing carrying a pocketbook like a woman, I mean a white woman? Did you steal it from your work madam, you nigger bitch? You thieving black bitch. I bet you niggers stole that car." Before they could taunt us further, Mom got back into the caddy and we sped away.

Approximately half a mile farther along we found our way blocked by an open-backed truck parked sideways across the road. As we pulled up, filled with uneasiness, the driver and the four men sitting in the back jumped out and started circling our car. A short man, with either a burn or a birthmark on the side of his face, grabbed the door handle on the driver's side and told us to get out. He said, "I've got some watermelon and fried chicken for you all in my truck. Clara had crouched down on the floor and shielded herself from view with a blanket. The racist taunts were profuse from the entire group, but the little man was the most foul. When he got rolling with his insults and intimidations, the others started to laugh and egg him on. His voice was pitched louder and higher as excitement overtook him. "You black shitty niggers, you wormy fucking nigger scum supposed to be crawling, but here you come in a white man's car. Let us see you buck dance. If we think you dance good enough, we might allow you all to crawl away from here. Dance niggers, dance!"

Mom got a desperately brilliant inspiration and proceeded to put it into action. She winked at us as she turned and slumped to the ground, then slowly got up doing a violent jerk-and-crouch, jerk-and-crouch. Her face was contorted, eyes bulging and tongue flicking like a serpent's. She let out a shriek and yelled, "Oh, Prince of Darkness, come to the aid of your faithful servant, Priestess of vengeance and pestilence. Smite those and their children who defy and berate Thee and me." She waved her arm at us the way she did when she wanted us to join in her song at church. We took the cue and started yelling with her: "Lucifer, Lucifer, oh Lucifer, before they die, make these vipers writhe and crawl on their bellies like the snakes they are! AHHHH—EEEEE—AH—."

The youngest-looking guy in the group stopped laughing and backed up slowly. The others looked from him to us, from us to him, and back again at us. The silence was pregnant for a second or two until Mom started up again. The faces changed. Squinted eyes opened wide in bewildered horror, and the mouths were no longer melon slices. Suddenly the young guy yelled, "Holy shit, Jess, them niggers is crazy. Aunt Jane putting a spell on us. I'm getting the fuck out of here." And that's exactly what they did. They got the fuck out of there.

We could only surmise that the men at the gas station had alerted the second group to watch for us as we headed in their direction. Luckily, we still had enough gas to put a little distance between us. We dared not stop until we were almost out of the next town and didn't want to stop there, but the tank was empty. That attendant was very pleasant, but we were still nervous. Even when we felt enough at ease to laugh about our performance, we took turns glancing at the road behind us.

The Atlanta program was all we had hoped it would be. We managed to tuck the road incident in our mental "forget file" and proceed with the business of enjoying Children's Day. Life was more bearable when we concentrated on the pleasant experiences. Regrettably, Negroes had great exercise sorting out what was to be tossed out of the conscious mind and onto the heap of degradation and injustice.

Obviously, though, remnants of that emotional roller coaster lingered in Clara's mind. Often, when we were discussing some other subject, she would interject her thoughts on hardship, injustice, brutality, and the inhumanity of slavery. "My Lord, those poor slaves," she would

say, moved to gentle, sympathetic tears, "they had to have been extremely strong emotionally and unshakable in their faith to face and
survive each new horrible day." Faith brought us all through personal
difficulties, and we had shared blessings as well, but the most fully and
deeply felt reflective moments were hers.

Clara often expressed her innermost thoughts in poetry or music. It
was in 1951—the same year of that experience in Georgia—that she
rewrote the spiritual, copyrighted, and recorded "How I Got Over."
Until her death, this song was Clara's rallying cry and, on occasion, her
salvation. When she sat humming the melody softly to herself, I would
almost always see in her eyes tiny pools reflecting the spirit of the ages.

*I*N 1952, my husband, who was doing maintenance work
wherever he could find it, was asked by my Aunt Clara to
give her fifteen-year-old grandson James some work to do
for the summer. John got a job to clean a shop floor. After much usage
and spillage, the old floor had become heavily stained and unsightly, so
John decided to strip the ugly wood planks with a gasoline scrub. No
one ever determined how it started, but soon the room was engulfed in
flames, burning James and my husband on their upper bodies. My little
cousin's burns were serious, but John's were more severe and extensive.
They both survived, I'm glad to say, but were left with multiple perma-
nent scars.

John really had a tough time of it. He spent seven weeks in the hospital just for stabilization and still longer for skin grafts. Just when we
thought he was out of the woods, he contracted hepatitis from a trans-
fusion of contaminated blood and was hospitalized for another six
weeks.

Luckily, just a year before, we had taken out accident insurance that
the *Philadelphia Sunday Bulletin* was offering for a mere ten cents a week.

It paid all the hospital bills. But young James was uninsured, so to cover his medical expenses Aunt Clara sued us for $3,000, which we paid off at $60 a month for a long time. Mom told us she was going to take up a collection in church for us and split the money between Aunt Clara and me. For a reason I don't recall, Mom and Aunt Clara got into an argument, which brought the aid to a halt.

Even after John was finally dismissed from the hospital, there was pain and swelling; he was quite weak and could not use his hands for another four months or so. Consequently, we were desperate for money. John's family helped us over the hump with many little kindnesses, and we were most grateful, but that was when I decided to try to get club work. It took some time; from 1952 to 1957 I called agents and went for interviews and auditions—to no avail. Not until 1957–58 did a group I had been rehearsing, the Gay Charmers, get a few jobs, but it was difficult to keep the girls together when the work was so sparse. Next I decided to try performing as a single, and again was turned down many times before agent Bernie Rothbard booked me into the Twenty-One Key Club. That happened in 1962.

When Mom first heard that I was trying to do nightclub work, she swore she was going to die. Yet she had been proud to have the Ward Singers become the first Gospel group to headline a show at New York's famous Apollo Theater, attended by the same partying people as those who frequented the clubs. I never understood how churchgoing folks—many of whom are notoriously intolerant—can make excuses for or ignore completely their own bad habits and indiscretions. They can be brutally vocal about sinners' behavior while participating in the same or worse acts. How do you measure the rate of sin? Even those who don't cheat, drink, smoke, or gamble may lie—or strike their children in anger. I know a few who use drugs or otherwise lead lives of questionable morality. I have mental lists of things I may do or absolutely will not do. My choices are my own, as are everyone's. Who am I, or who are they, to choose what is all right for a Christian to do? We are humans—not gods. We do the best we can.

Once I did start working in nightclubs—happy to be helping with household finances—I got an unexpectedly personal dose of "righteous" intolerance. John and his family were members of Thankful Baptist Church in Philadelphia. I had been happy worshiping at Mutchmore Memorial, but being the dutiful wife, I joined Thankful as my husband requested. We were quickly immersed in its activities. My girls sang in the children's choirs; John was on the ushers' board, and we both sang in the adult choir. I taught Ward songs to the vocal group the Trappaires and played the piano for them.

The week after I opened my first solo club act, however, I showed up at church for choir practice, only to be stunned when the group's president, Carrie Gervin, announced, "Willa, I must ask you to leave. Your presence here can only hurt the church."

"Okay," I said, "I'll stop playing for the choir."

"No," she said, "I mean you must leave the church for good." I ran out crying.

John, the girls, and I decided that before asking to join another church, we would tell the pastor what had happened to us and why. At Zion Baptist at Broad and Venango Streets, the Reverend Leon Howard Sullivan said, after hearing our story, "Some of my dearest friends—like Louis Armstrong and Lena Horne—are in show business. There is nothing wrong with the work you are doing as long as you don't degrade yourself or practice bad habits. You are welcome here." We each got a hug, and we knew we had found a church home. The next Sunday, he welcomed us from the pulpit.

This dear man is the same Leon Sullivan who built Zion Baptist's membership from five hundred to five thousand. *Life* magazine cited him among its one hundred outstanding young adults of 1963. He also founded the now international self-help Opportunities Industrialization Centers, taking his good work all over the world before his retirement.

Eventually, Mrs. Trapp, wife of the minister at Thankful Baptist Church, implored me to come back to their congregation. For me, the time for that had passed.

*W*E WORKED the Apollo Theater in Harlem fifteen times. The Philadelphia Davis Sisters, recording star James Cleveland, Charles Taylor, the Dixie Hummingbirds, and Billy Preston were on the first all-Gospel show that we headlined there. (Later, the 'Birds and Billy did crossover work with Paul Simon and the Beatles, respectively.)

There were four shows a day, which was tiring enough, but even when not performing we had to sit on stage for the duration of each show. The intention was to simulate a churchlike atmosphere where the excitement mounts—with ample stimulation from all the folks present, including other performers and the audience.

I was so exhausted, I sometimes skipped a show. Mom had added Ethel Gilbert and Gloria Griffin (of the Roberta Martin Singers) to our group just for that Apollo stint, so the sound was still full without me. Poor Clara was beat, too, but dared not miss a performance. She dipped heavily into the bottle to make it through. She would sit on stage completely dropped out until it was time for her to sing herself back to consciousness. Most of the time I was her "bag lady," carrying Clara's booze in my handbag to keep Mom from finding it in hers.

When we were on a mixed bill, we were allowed to socialize with other Gospel singers, but Mom absolutely forbade our fraternizing with the "devils" of the show business world, even though in our brief encounters they always treated us respectfully—with minor exceptions. Every Saturday the Apollo had a midnight show after the four regular ones, which found the entertainers struggling to hold up. They made the long day seem less taxing by socializing backstage.

One time we were working a show with two glorious singers, Arthur Prysock and Gloria Lynne. My sister and I were thrilled with their individual talents but of course hid our enjoyment from Mom—who disallowed our joining the others in their merriment. Our orders were to stay in our dressing room unless we had to go on stage or to the ladies' room. We could hear the delicious laughter rushing in waves from the hall. Just the infectious tone of it made us smile and giggle, even though we had no idea what precipitated it.

Then Honi Coles, a magnificent tap dancer who was between gigs and working as stage manager, came into our dressing room to ask why we weren't out with the others. Being our truthful little selves, we told him why. "You're grown women," he shouted. "Your mother's out there in the thick of the crowd while you dummies sit in this cube like Mickey Mouses. It's hard to believe in this day and age there's some chicken asses like you two." We knew he was right as we stared in silence at the door he had just closed—but knowing what was truth didn't end our Mom-imposed segregation.

When our time came to sing, we emerged from the tiny room to be greeted by the show's comedian, Dusty Fletcher, who drawled in a slow, deliberate voice, "Well hello there, I do believe we have among us the two and only M and M Sisters." The stifled laughter from the gallery cut us to the quick. We got on the stage and blew their laughter up their noses.

MANY OF my most memorable experiences happened while I was in New York for Apollo engagements and others. One was when "the lights went out in Harlem"—and the rest of the city. I had gone downtown between shows to see booking agent Jolly Joyce about a possible tour with Rosetta Tharpe. On my way back uptown, as I walked down the subway steps, all the lights died. I ran back up the stairs to find the streets and buildings dark also, and people milling about in confusion.

I managed to get on a jam-packed uptown bus and walked the rest of the way after getting off at the stop nearest the theater. They had small auxiliary lights and candles working in the Apollo when I got back. We sat on stage in candlelight till eleven but didn't sing because there was no power for amplification. Clara and I thought the whole thing was fun—until we had to walk up to the fourteenth floor of our hotel to reach our room. On our way to the stairs we looked through the open door of the hotel's bar. It looked so cozy and inviting we were tempted to go in and sit down in the candlelit room, but we were afraid Mom would find out.

Another Apollo stint found us in New York when a snowstorm developed so fast and copiously that we were forced to spend the night in the theater. We sang and played long after show time was over. It turned into a jubilant session.

Speaking of jubilation, what a marvelous time we had singing spirituals and hymns with "the King," Elvis Presley, at a rehearsal for the *Ed Sullivan Show*. He loved Clara and started calling her "Little Sister." All the people who heard Clara and Elvis singing together—a cappella, with the rest of us harmonizing and clapping—thought it was wonderful. Elvis agreed that the sound was worth recording and approached his manager, "Colonel" Tom Parker, with the proposal. Later, Elvis told Clara that the Colonel dismissed the idea because some of Elvis's fans might not approve of the race mix, even if it was only "recorded integration." About a month after that, Clara received a gorgeous bolt of gold-sequined material from the King.

Again we were rehearsing for an appearance on Sullivan's show a few years later when we were shocked senseless. Earlier, on the train churning to New York City, Clara and I had shared thoughts on where we came from and where we were headed—two "little girls" from North Philadelphia on our way to be shown off to the world—again. We were just getting our music set up for the band when an excited young man bolted in, arms flailing, and yelled, "The President's been shot! President Kennedy has been shot!" The entire crew was in pandemonium. Someone got a radio and turned it on to the news that plunged us all into deep despair. Understandably, Sullivan canceled that rehearsal and show.

On the way home we encountered many people joined in grief, expressing emotions that turned liquid in the form of silent, gentle tears or copious sobs. I walked into my house back in Philadelphia to find my husband sitting in a darkened room in front of the television set, crying his heart out. We didn't speak. I just slid into his arms and there we sat entwined in a mourning embrace, grieving for our beloved president.

E HAD always thought of New York's Carnegie Hall as a place where the world's renowned classical artists performed until, on an October Sunday afternoon in 1950, the Famous Ward singers became a part of the great hall's history. We starred with our friend the great Mahalia Jackson in a Gospel program produced and emcee'd by the prominent New York promoter and disk jockey Joe Bostic, of radio station WLIB. Mahalia sang "It Pays to Serve Jesus," "The Last Mile of the Way," "Amazing Grace," and her trademark "Move on up a Little Higher." When our turn came, we planted our new, shiny shoes on the shiny wooden floor, arched our backs like divas, and gave our all to "Each Day" and "Come Ye Disconsolate" (featuring the trio of Clara, Marion Williams, and me). The entire group then did "Stretch Out" and "Surely God Is Able." Our first Carnegie Hall appearance was a resounding success.

The full program also included contralto Ruth Stewart, who sang the national anthem to the capacity crowd; the Belleville (Virginia) Acapella Choir; faith healer and psychic reader Mother McClease; the Angel Lites, "world's youngest Gospel group"; radio and television star Lorenzo Fuller, from the cast of the Broadway musical *Kiss Me, Kate*; Little Reverend Donald Gay—a four-year-old preacher from Chicago— assisted by Evelyn and Mildred Gay; and the Reverend Adam Clayton Powell Jr., a U.S. Congressman and pastor of the Abyssinian Baptist Church (at that time, the world's largest Protestant congregation).

Grace Kelly came to hear us—the first of many times—when she was studying acting at a school around the corner from Carnegie Hall. She and her friends came backstage and introduced themselves to us. Everyone in our group was struck by her loveliness. She was soft yet came on loud and strong by just standing there looking like a queen. We were not surprised that she later became a princess. It was fitting.

Grace later introduced us to her boyfriend, who worked with the William Morris theatrical booking agency. He begged us to sign a contract to sing pop music with a guarantee of megabucks. We were certain Mom would reject the offer, but even we were taken aback by her utter disdain and wild outburst. "John Hyde," she screamed, "you're trying to tear down all I've built up. You're the Devil's Disciple! You hear me, you're the Devil's Disciple!" Luckily, though stunned, Hyde took Mom's tirade in stride. This man was obviously a professional who had seen and heard it all. He made it clear that his efforts were about making money, not making friends of Gospel singers.

Ironically, it was John Hyde who had booked the first gospel singer into Carnegie Hall when, in 1938, Rosetta Tharpe appeared on a program called "From Spirituals to Swing," featuring a mix of jazz and spirituals, Gospel and blues. Performing in the company of secular singers did not appear to have hurt Rosetta any. That same year her recording with Lucky Millinder's band of Thomas A. Dorsey's "Hide Me in Thy Bosom," under the title "Rock Me," was a huge national hit.

John Hyde wasn't at all interested in handling us as a Gospel group, but he did arrange for us to appear on *Those Ragtime Years*, a television special on which Honi Coles and his partner Cholly Alkins did buck dancing, the cakewalk, step-tapping, and more—a chronology of dances created by blacks. Musicians and songwriters Eubie Blake and Hoagie Carmichael played ragtime piano with abundant amounts of their own original magnificence thrown in. Popular TV and movie personality Dorothy Loudon was on the show too. We all dressed in period clothing; the Ward Singers were convincing as plantation fieldhands in long cotton dresses, aprons, and square-tied head bandannas. Our kind of Gospel singing did not belong to the early 1900s, so we did authentic traditional hymns and spirituals. We did many television shows after that, yet we performers received little remuneration for most of them. When *Those Ragtime Years* was aired again, residual fees were paid, but I didn't get anything. Mom kept telling us the exposure was all we should expect; whatever money there was went into promotion and agent or manager payments.

It was also John Hyde who introduced us to manager Fred Strauss, booking agent Monte Kay, and publicity agent Virginia Wicks. When we signed with them to handle the business end of the Ward Singers, it freed Mom to concentrate on designing wardrobe and our now famous coiffures. Fred and Monte took 10 percent off the top of all job money; Virginia Wicks got a flat $150 each week.

By the late 1950s we had really moved up financially—on paper. But the money never filtered down to us proportionally. Enough did sift through the promotional net, however, to pay for a custom, $14,000 nine-passenger limo built by Chrysler and an official chauffeur, Rudy Scott.

We had also added two new members who greatly enhanced the Ward Singers' sound. Kitty Parham came out of a church choir in Jamaica, New York, and brought with her a voice that had no frills or hooks, just total integrity in singing Gospel. The one and only female bass singer, Frances Steadman from Baltimore, put a bottom to our group that no other woman could have duplicated. Her voice ran deep and cool as the waters that feed an artesian well.

THE *Pittsburgh Courier* Theatrical Poll was a nationwide ranking of performers and entertainment in various categories, determined annually by write-in votes from the public. Voters could select anyone they wished that fit the slots.

Clara Ward and the Famous Ward Singers won the Gospel music category hands down in 1952, 1953, and 1954. As the *Courier's* report of the award ceremony put it:

Clara Ward, director and pianist for the nationally famous Ward Singers, is not just soloist for the Ward Singers, but stands out as one of the greatest gospel soloists of all times. This versatile young woman arranges, writes and publishes gospel music which is sung by singers all over America. Clara Ward, about whom the great Ward Singers revolve, has won over the great Mahalia Jackson, who came in a distant second.

The list of winners in 1952 shows how many votes separated first from second place in each category.

Category	Name	Votes More Than Next Highest
Gospel singers	The Ward Singers	48,000
Vocal quartet	The Ravens	1,650
Female singer (pop)	Delores Brown	7,340
Female singer (blues)	Ruth Brown	31,660
Male singer (pop)	Arthur Prysock	5,250
Male singer (blues)	Nickey Lee	3,060
Big band	Buddy Johnson	2,720
Small band combo	The Ray-O-Vacs	—
Trio (instrumental)	Nat King Cole	3,060
Movie	*Sudden Fear* with Joan Crawford	1,100
School or college band	Bethune-Cookman College (Daytona Beach, Florida)	2,140
Movie star	Dorothy Dandridge	1,740
T.V. show	*I Love Lucy*	1,090
Radio show	*Dragnet*	1,090
New talent	Jean Dunn (singer)	890

Among those voted most popular in 1953 were Sarah Vaughan, Dinah Washington, Billy Eckstein, Count Basie, Lionel Hampton, Ella Fitzgerald, Joe Williams, and the Ward Singers—we won our category by a huge margin again.

Soon after that we had a show at Philadelphia Convention Hall, where 13,700 attended. No hall was big enough to accommodate all the masses that so graciously took the money and time to see and hear us. At this writing, I don't know any Gospel group that could pull in the crowds we did. We had to do the Newark Armory twice that year because the first show was sold out. The second drew 11,000 more.

OM WAS constantly getting pleas from people seeking her successful formula for promoting a program, and Clara was deluged with requests for words and music to her original material. The people got what they wanted on both counts.

My mother wrote a booklet giving step-by-step details of how to do a program and suggestions on what to avoid. The booklet was issued free of charge to anyone who requested it and sent a self-addressed stamped envelope.

Among her instructions were these:

DO'S FOR PROMOTERS

1. Have artists people want to hear, especially those whose records are being played on the air.

2. Get a church or auditorium big enough to hold the people.

3. Print tickets, throwouts, and placards to be given out at other concerts and programs; place placards on poles and in stores, churches, and homes.

4. Place tickets on sale in churches, in record shops, and with church members, and give 10 percent to ticket sellers.

5. Announce program on all Gospel radio stations and in newspapers.

DON'TS FOR USHERS

Don't be unpleasant, in words or actions, when meeting those coming in or going out of worship.

Don't be in too big a hurry in dealing with people who ask for information or help. Remember, you are an *usher*, not a *rusher*.

Don't forget that your haughtiness, dumbness, or unfriendly ways will drive away *souls* that are hungry and looking for *God*. If you meet and greet them friendly . . . they will most likely come again. By your *courtesy*, *kindness*, and *winning smile*, you may be instrumental in bringing *souls to Christ!*

DON'TS FOR CHOIRS, QUARTETS, CHORAL GROUPS, AND GOSPEL SINGERS

Don't forget that the world will not be saved by halfhearted service. Put all you have into it. Your singing is *"Praising God from Whom All Blessings Flow."*

Don't neglect *prayer* and *consecration!*

Don't think that a good voice, alone, will make a good singer. You must have *character, good common sense,* and that *good, heartfelt religion.*

Don't think that your *high* voice range will substitute for *high-tone moral character.* High voice and low life may make a good blues singer, but *not* a good Gospel singer.

Don't think you can sing well without rehearsal—*"Practice still makes perfect."*

CLARA'S RESPONSE was more elaborate. In 1953 she opened Ward's House of Music in the basement of a property that she and Mom bought at 18th and Butler Streets. They lived on the first and second floors and rented out the third.

Among music publishing businesses across the country, precious few expressly handled compositions by and geared to blacks. Traditionally, spirituals and hymns arranged or composed by Europeans or white Americans were the music sung by choirs and congregations in the black church. When Gospel came into favor, the need was acute for ways to get this wonderful music legitimized and out to the people. The Reverend C. A. Tindley had worn the two hats of composer and publisher, but he published only his own works. The National Baptist Convention U.S.A., Inc. however, which introduced new Gospel songs to conventioneers each year, also began to produce song collections and sheet music. As need and rapidly expanding market demanded, a few other Gospel composers and singers opened their own publishing companies—among them Roberta Martin, Sallie Martin and Kenneth Morris, Lillian Bowles and Theodore Frye—chiefly in Chicago.

Ward's House of Music first put out only sheet music (at twenty cents) but added songbooks (fifty cents) as the volume of material and the orders expanded. The music we published came from various sources. Clara was hitting her creative stride, and besides her work and the Reverend W. H. Brewster's, others brought original material for us to process; we paid $50 per song for all rights. The Davis Sisters of Philadelphia were churning out songs so fast that they were often quite rough, or so slight that we combined several into one. Our arrangers—Dorothy Pearson, Berisford Shepherd, Mary Wiley, and Mr. Jones—would polish and buff the edges of lyrics and music until the finished pieces displayed the qualities we wanted to produce.

I managed the operation, handling all details of selecting, compiling, and order-filling. We sent out circulars to other stores and performers, announcing new songs and offering discount rates for large quantities. We also did business with other black Gospel publishers and exchanged material with them, thus expanding our output even further.

In 1963 we opened a second music house at 23rd Street and Columbia Avenue (now Cecil B. Moore Avenue) and added records and greeting cards to our stock of printed music. (Mom didn't know it, but I sold secular as well as religious records there.) I hired Martha Bass as sales manager of the new store, but the effort was still too great, and we had to close it after two years.

My father helped with the packing and shipping, and handling shipments that often totaled 20,000 pieces took its toll on both of us. Pop was plagued with chronic sprainlike symptoms in both wrists and his lower back. I developed a tumor where my thumb met the string from the many, many bundles; I had it removed twice.

Mom and Clara stayed on the road twenty-two months of the first two years after opening Ward's House of Music, coming home only for

Christmas and Easter. I would send them as many pieces as they requested for sale wherever they were singing. None of the money from those sales was sent back to me for operational costs; it meant pure profit for them. I was paid $50 a week, but Pop was not salaried. Mom said I was to give him a few bucks as he needed it (and she really meant "a few"). How humiliating that must have been for him. Mom was really tight when it came to parting with money—except when it was used for her whims; she very often squandered her own and Clara's money on frivolities, as I learned in detail later.

Clara wanted to move into the third-floor apartment over the House of Music. She longed for a place of her own where she could relax without Mom's ever watchful—and vocal—presence. My sister was at the point where she needed some normal life as an adult, freedom to entertain guests of her own choosing and to regulate the off hours that were hers. But Mom, true to form, rejected the idea as foolish and wasteful. "You don't need to be by yourself. Somebody could come in and do you harm—besides we need the rent money," she told a very disappointed Clara. Little did it matter that Clara's talent and hard work had paid for the property, and two others as well.

CLARA'S BUDDING romance with C. L. Franklin rapidly developed into flower. They found loving easy—the difficult part was keeping the sweet aroma of *amour* from Mom's sensitive nose. A plan was devised to allow the lovers to spend some quality and continuous time together. Although Mom was jealous of Clara's closeness to C.L., she liked his children well enough, which made her receptive to the idea of Clara's traveling to Detroit to sit with them occasionally. If she knew that the good Reverend was doing most of the sitting—and more—with my sister Clara, she did not let on.

There was mutual adoration between Clara and the Franklin children—Erma, Cecil, and Aretha. They loved being together, talking, laughing, and singing. Those times provided all of them with a feeling of being a complete family.

Clara was so amazed by Aretha's singing voice and delivery that she offered all the guidance she could to advance that huge talent. Aretha had an inherent gift from Mother Africa or Mother Earth, a gift that increased in value with every passing day. No one could have taught her how to reach back up to where heart joins soul, gather the treasures trembling there, and then, song by song, present her glory to the listening world. Here was this shy, unaffected child who could without plan yank the covers off folks' emotions.

As Clara's "babysitting" trips became more frequent and lengthy, Mom got more and more perturbed and was bent on turning things around. Over and over again she told Clara, "Franklin just wants you to build his congregation up. You've come too far and worked too hard to be singing there for free." In fact, Franklin's New Bethel Baptist Church in Detroit had a healthy membership of 4,600, so it was hardly in need of a parishioner drive. Folks came from all over Detroit to attend the church's services; even nonmembers really piled in on those days when the Reverend Franklin, who was a fine singer as well as a powerful preacher, included familiar material from his popular records, especially "The Eagle Stirs Her Nest." Still, without question, when Clara was there, her contribution enhanced the services greatly. With little Aretha's solo thrown in for good measure, those programs were happenings.

The meeting of the World Baptist Alliance, a prestigious annual gathering of the faithful from around the globe, was coming up in July 1955 in Europe. Mom had already told us she had no plans to attend, and that made the idea of going—as tourists, not performers—highly appealing to Clara and C.L. The couple was very careful not to book any programs that would conflict with the convention schedule. For weeks, secret preparations were in the works.

"I can't believe it, I can't believe it," Clara kept repeating over and over again when she and Franklin finally had plans and reservations for a trip to Europe and the Holy Land all firmed up. Interspersed with all that joy, however, was great fear of Mom's reaction to the news. We worked feverishly on verbal tactics that might cushion the dreaded ordeal. We decided on a direct approach, which my poor sister practiced again and again. But her nerve and confidence needed constant boosting; she was a wreck.

The Reverend Franklin was a great help. He reinforced Clara's spirits when she became weak and held her up when fear just about collapsed her. Finally, dwindling time dictated telling Gertrude—and it was done! Mom's opposition was obvious but not to the extent we had all anticipated. I guess she recognized that it was time to bend a little or lose Clara completely to the rest of the world—C. L. Franklin's world.

Newspeople, friends, and family saw Clara and C.L. board the Air France plane that took them on the first leg of their journey to three continents and eleven countries. When they returned the person deplaning from the Paris flight behind the Reverend Franklin was a confident, smiling woman with gentle, expressive eyes. Instantly, I could see that my sister was more together than when she left. She even looked taller as she floated down the steps of the airplane. Photographers' flashbulbs were going off, and reporters hurled questions at Clara the minute her feet reconnected with American soil. She asked them to be courteous enough to let the other passengers pass and said she would make a statement in the terminal. I think even Franklin was impressed as Clara finally turned to the assembled people, raised her arm for the silence she immediately got, and said (in part):

> As a gospel singer, constantly extolling Jesus in song to millions of Americans, I had always harbored a dream of going to the Holy Land, of seeing firsthand the places where Jesus and those before Him and with Him lived.
>
> In July of this year, I attended the World Baptist Alliance, which met in London. While I enjoyed London and Paris, my mind kept tugging me to my dream—the Holy Land. When I reached the land where Christ walked, the ancient settings struck me with electric realization. To think that here are the places of which I sing! Here is where He lived, prayed, and died!
>
> I am anxious to tell the world of my great inspiration—of how I as a Ward Singer will sing better than ever because of it. Although two thousand years have passed since Jesus made the burdened, dragging,

suffering climb to Calvary, I walked up the same path and felt as if it were happening at the moment and I was there. Slowly I retraced His steps. My heart cried out when I touched the spot where He first fell. I was glad when Simon helped Him with the cross. I rejoiced when the Daughters of Zion wiped His sweaty, bloody face. I followed His weary trail up the incline to Calvary where He was nailed to the cross. My heart ached. My mind rushed back to the other places I had visited—where He too had been two thousand years ago. I had prayed in the Garden of Gethsemane where Jesus had prayed, and I felt His despair and suffering. I had actually stood in the judgment hall, where Pontius Pilate washed his hands, trying to wash the blame of killing Jesus from them. I had been atop the Mountain of Temptation where Jesus fasted and prayed. I had seen the places where He taught, the gate through which He rode into Jerusalem, and the place where He said, "The Son of Man hath no place to lay his head."

No one will understand how close I felt to Him as I saw Old Cairo, where Mary hid Jesus from avenging Herod for three months; and the place where the angel Gabriel appeared to Mary and told her about the coming birth of Christ. I washed my hands in the great River Jordan where Christ was baptized. I visited the humble home of Mary and Joseph in Nazareth where they lived with Jesus after returning from Egypt. I followed Jesus with a song in my heart. I followed Him to Cana in Galilee where He turned water into wine at a wedding, to the site of the Sermon on the Mount and the place where the multitudes were fed with two fish and five loaves of bread, then on to where He had His last supper. I placed my hand on the stone that had blocked His tomb and was rolled away by the angels.

The fullness in me overflowed into tears as I sat beside the Sea of Galilee or stood on the ground where Jesus was nailed to the cross. I was uplifted at Mount Olive where Jesus Christ ascended into Heaven. It was glorious! These sites where Christ had lived, taught, and suffered moved my soul, and I knew that when I returned to America, as the newly inspired Clara, I would perform with a more profound understanding and appreciation of my Lord Jesus Christ.

As it turned out, this was the only vacation my sister ever had.

*T*HROUGHOUT most of the 1950s our anniversary programs continued to be the major events that drew large
crowds. On our seventeenth anniversary, once the musical
selections and participants were set, Mom chose the green gowns with se-
quin trim as our outfits for the evening's celebration. As Kitty Parham, Esther Ford, Frances Steadman, Marion Williams, my cousin Marguerite
Shaw, and I were dressing, we all stared in disbelief when Mom and Clara
opened their garment bags. They took out two gorgeous, billowing
gowns—the kind Scarlett O'Hara wore in the last scenes of *Gone with the
Wind*, beautiful new garments designed to set them apart from the rest of
us—me included. There was nothing subtle about this new wedge between Clara, Mom, and me. Even though I had shared in each and every
hardship the original Ward Singers had endured, it was evident I was not
to share fully in the successes. By now I was just another dispensable
singer. Even though Mom tried to appease my anger by allowing me to
sing "The Lord's Prayer" as a solo (which incidentally received a tremendous ovation), I knew a time would come when there would be no such
gestures offered—no pretense worth the effort.

For our twenty-first anniversary, Ethel Gilbert replaced Marguerite Shaw, and David Riddick took Clara's place at the piano so
that she could move around and join in the "holy dance." Mom
wanted this one to be extra special, and it was. As always, our guest
lineup included some of the most outstanding names in Gospel, many
of whom had appeared on other Ward anniversaries and programs.
This particular grouping—the Harmonizing Four, Sammy Bryant, the
Roberta Martin Singers, Sister Wynona Carr, the CBS Trumpeters,
and C. L. Franklin, in addition to the Ward Singers—was dynamite. We heated the atmosphere up so I'd be surprised if the radia-
tion didn't scorch the Pearly Gates. Over twenty-thousand jubilant
listeners became participants and shouted the evening away with their
praises. When Clara sang her gold-record hit, "Surely God Is Able,"

the ushers and nurses had to administer to hundreds of folks overcome with emotion.

On our twenty-fourth anniversary program at the Philadelphia Arena in 1957, we presented not only a stellar lineup of soloists and groups but a hundred-voice chorus made up of still other prominent Gospel singers. It was another "first" for the Ward Singers.

 Y SISTER could churn out a new song in a few hours or chew on one for days and days. She drew inspiration from every source imaginable, and her career as a composer and recording artist was really taking off. By the mid-1950s she had recorded some fifty singles and albums; many more would follow. The magnitude of such an accomplishment, understandably, began to breed a measure of independence. I thoroughly encouraged all Clara's attempts, however feeble, to become a whole person. Mom knew this and so warned my sister that listening to me and Reverend Franklin would lead to her immediate downfall. Mom seemed to sense that her ironfisted grip on Clara's every thought and movement was slipping. She used numerous ploys to halt the slippage, including guilt. She would lament "I've sacrificed and done everything I could to put you on top and this is the thanks I get—that's all right, I'll get my reward in Heaven. Or, "This ol' body is plum worn out trying to do for you and others. You'll all miss me when I'm gone. See how good you'll do without me."

We giggled and joked behind Mom's back about her dramatics, but even as Clara smiled and seemed to make light of the situation, it was evident that her defenses were cracking. What finally reconverted my sister into the puppet she had been before her trip abroad was the contrived or actual mental change that caused Mom to behave peculiarly. She began ranting about seeing and speaking with spirits that promised to ward off all troubles or create some for anyone who crossed or angered her. With the spirits on Mom's side, my poor sister felt powerless to challenge her and her supernatural allies; consequently, Clara's acquiescence was complete in short order. The poor little lamb was whipped to shreds, completely shorn of self-control. The only things that Clara had for her solace were singing the Gospel and slurping the booze. My sister said to me, "The only way I can survive is to drink. If I didn't, Mom would drive me crazy or give me a heart attack. God help me." This pitiful declaration lay in my stomach like lead.

JAZZ BUFFS from all over the world eagerly attend the Newport (Rhode Island) Jazz Festival each year. Nineteen fifty-seven was the very first year Gospel was added to what had previously been strictly a jazz format.

Being invited to appear on the show was like being asked by the celestial trumpeter Gabriel to jam with the Heavenly All-Stars (no sacrilege intended). What a pleasure to be sharing the stage with such musical giants as Dionne Warwick and the Drinkard Singers, Eartha Kitt, Duke Ellington, Billie Holiday, Mahalia Jackson, Dave Brubeck, and Louis Armstrong. We had met them all before except Dave Brubeck and Eartha Kitt. Eartha was a pleasant surprise to us. We had mistakenly assumed that she was aloof and arrogant, but her warmth and cordiality were infectious.

Poor Billie Holiday, who died just two years later, was on her last legs. Seeing her struggle to push the pitiful sounds from her throat and past her quivering lips made my eyes well up with tears. That was the last time I saw "the Lady" alive. I've often wished I had given her a hug and some encouraging words (though I have no idea what I might have said) to ease the dread of the impending doom she must have felt.

*T*N 1958 my father finally went on a tour with us. It began in Richmond, Virginia, with a program celebrating the Harmonizing Four's anniversary, who with Rosetta Tharpe and the Ward Singers (all booked by Mom on this run) made a joyful noise that night. The next day we headed out, caravan style, on a circuitous route to California via Chicago, Kansas City, Wichita, and Denver.

On this trip my cousin Mary Simmons chauffeured us in our recently acquired twelve-passenger Chrysler limousine, which was luxurious and ultracomfortable. Actually, the car itself afforded us the only comfort connected with our travel, for Mom forbade us to smoke, listen to the radio, or engage in any lengthy conversation with each other. The only relief came when we ate, slept, or sang.

In Chicago we sang on the television show *In Town Tonight*, hosted by Irv Kupcinet. After the show, Marion Williams, who was pregnant, became ill and was worse the next day. Fearing complications, she decided to return to Philadelphia.

Illness struck again in Wichita, Kansas, the hometown of Lillie Mae, a new singer who had joined us in Richmond. She had recently had a hysterectomy and was told by her physician not to engage in sex for five weeks. Not following that professional advice, she put her life in jeopardy by doing the wild thing. By the time we were ready to leave town, Lillie had a high fever and was bleeding profusely. Although we tried to get her to seek the medical help she so desperately needed, she refused to see a doctor or leave her house. Mom prayed with her for almost an hour, asking "Dr. Jesus" to take Lillie's case.

Time eventually ran out—we had to leave. Lillie managed to drag herself to the door to watch us take off. The last we saw of her was a wistful smile that barely spread her fever-parched lips and a reluctant arm waving in slow motion. We all started crying and praying for Lillie Mae. The following day, when Mom called to check on her condition, the landlady said that The Master had interceded and taken His child into His care. Lillie Mae had just died.

WE WERE THE FIRST Gospel group to sing at the Los Angeles Paramount Theatre. The usual performers there were big bands, jazz groups, and singers such as Patti Page, Frank Sinatra, Tony Bennett, and Ray Charles, so seeing our names up on the marquee was thrilling. The *Los Angeles Times* for April 25, 1958, carried a glowing review of our performance. In part, it read:

> The most striking of their numbers . . . was "Let's Get Ready for That Great Day," in which Clara Ward's crystal soprano soared so high, so sweet, and so angel trumpet clear over the tremulous, earthy altos of her companions that the true eschatological meaning of the song was suggested more powerfully than this reviewer can do justice to.

Another reporter said that one woman who was dressed in a flowing orange robe made the greatest impression vocally. "Let's Get Ready for That Great Day" was a song that I had written, originally titled "Who Shall Be Able to Stand." I always sang it, and I was the only one wearing an orange robe. But our promotional flyers positioned that tribute under Clara's picture, suggesting that it had been written about her. I got no credit for the comment or for the song.

Rosetta begged me to leave the Wards and tour with her through Europe. She and Fred Strauss, who had booked us into the Paramount (and later booked my group into nightclubs), both thought we would be sensational together. The more I thought about it, the more the thought appealed to me. I called my husband, but he immediately rejected the proposition, even though the financial reward would have been great.

It was some compensation that our first visit to Disneyland was so much fun. I had never seen my father that loose or imagined him as a youth until then. Mom kept telling him to act his age, but for a brief magic moment Daddy stripped away the ravages of hardships, agonies, and time and gleefully became again the smiling, gangly young boy from South Carolina (I'm sure he had almost forgotten).

LSO IN 1958, with Esther Ford, Kitty Parham, Henrietta Waddy, Frances Steadman, Marion Williams, Mom, Clara, and me, and David Riddick playing the organ, we had our last anniversary. (Actually, we did celebrate a few more, but after 1958 circumstances altered the concept drastically. The group that Clara and Mom had molded into what they thought would be a lasting unit was soon to be fractured.) Last but not lacking, our twenty-fifth was a grand success. Ten thousand people filled the Philadelphia Arena to capacity, and at least another thousand were lined up outside, still hoping to get in.

That same year we also appeared on our first national television shows: *Today,* with hosts Betsy Palmer and the witty and warm Dave Garroway, and Steve Allen's very popular *Tonight.* (Eventually, the Wards did the Steve Allen show twice, *Today* seven times, and the Mike Douglas show fifteen times.) One of our singers who was five minutes late for the *Tonight* rehearsal drew the ire and hot lips of Ma Gert. She singled out the tardy singer for special attention but gave us all a lengthy cursing out for mistakes past and a warning that we would get more of the same in the future if we weren't careful. Everyone in the studio witnessed our embarrassment.

The jobs and television shows were coming in rapidly, yet we singers were still not being compensated fairly. After coming off a short tour we were scheduled to do the *Today* show again. The day before, Marion called Mom and told her that she, Kitty, Frances, Esther, and Henrietta would not be showing up and that the five of them were leaving the group. We did the show with our few remaining singers, but the results were pitiful. We had to get the Imperials with Anna Smallwood to fill our bookings until we could regroup—which we did. Our shock and feeling of betrayal were soon replaced by renewed faith and determination to "overcome." Mom kept saying, "Sometimes things happen for the best. Leave it in the hands of the Lord."

Strauss, who was still also booking Mom and Clara. Although our records for Savoy never moved, our appearances in nightclubs throughout the tristate area and Canada were quite successful. (I continued working in duos until 1991.)

When agent Bernie Lowe asked me to get some female singers together to sing background for various recording artists, John was against the idea, saying that to do so would detract from creative and rehearsal time with the Gay Charmers. I am so glad that for once I defied him and put together the group known (for a brief period) as the Willettes. We found backup work plentiful and rewarding. We got to do different kinds of arrangements with some great people, and the money helped to put my girls through college. Rita went to Voorhees Junior College in Denmark, South Carolina, and Charlotte and Rita both attended Hampton Institute in Hampton, Virginia. (When they were babies, Mom had told me that if I went on the road to sing with the group, she would help put my girls through college. Those were empty words. The only things she provided were a foot locker for Rita and a suitcase and television set for Charlotte.)

John was still determined to be father, agent, manager, conscience, and all to everyone I worked with. He tried to monitor all our comings and goings, to influence our yeas and nays. During that period I was doing club work, recording, and concerts, and maybe we came and went more than was necessary. But many really good jobs were cut short because John missed me. Sometimes we had to come home just when options were being picked up—because he missed me. It was so unfair to all of us except John that after a while Doris got disgusted and left. Shortly thereafter she married an Englishman we had met while working the Black Orchid in Montreal.

Another coworker I lost because of John was Toni Rose, a drummer and singer. She and I teamed up and developed some dynamite arrangements for a vast repertoire. We were on the move upward and outward. One job we had, in Lake George, New York, offered juicy side benefits. The pay was fabulous, and our contract was extended to last the entire summer. Our home away from home was a bungalow with two bedrooms, sitting room, kitchen, bath, and a Florida room with beautiful greenery and a baby grand piano in the center. It was nestled in stately pine trees at the base of a green mountain and just two blocks from a beautiful lake (one of many). To top it off, we had a yacht and its captain at our disposal. Toni was absolutely furious when, after working at the club just three of the thirteen weeks scheduled, I told her we had to leave because John wanted me home. The end of our collaboration came after my husband canceled our Greenland and European tours. Exit Toni Rose.

WHEN I was recruiting for my background group, I advertised in the *Philadelphia Daily News*, *Tribune*, and *Bulletin* for singers who could sight-read music. The few who answered the ads could not do so to my satisfaction—with one exception: fifteen-year-old Dee Dee Sharp breezed through the test music like a pro. Dee Dee's grandfather was a minister who vehemently objected to his granddaughter's singing secular music, but fortunately for Dee Dee, her mother and the rest of the family overruled him. I drew up a contract naming me as her manager, and she and Doris Gibson and I went on recording sessions doing background for Cameo records. Kal Mann, Russ Faith, and Dave Appell, who ran that company, had written a song for Chubby Checker, their star performer, as a follow-up to his big hit "Let's Do the Twist." They zeroed in on Dee Dee as the girl they wanted to make up a duo with Chubby. I urged her to seize the moment and sold her contract to Cameo. Russ, Kal, and Dave wasted little time; within a month, Checker and Sharp's "Slow Twisting" was on its way to becoming a smash hit that topped the charts. The transaction aided us in paying off bills and in purchasing the house I still own and live in.

As the rock-and-roll industry heated up in the late 1950s and early 1960s, backup singers were in high demand, for we had the sound and drive everyone was looking for. Vivian Dix, Blanche Norton, Mary Wiley, Dee Dee Sharp, and I had a big pushing sound that jammed and filled the harmonic spaces for popular singers such as Screamin' Jay Hawkins, Dion, Nickey Demateo, Fabian, Frankie Avalon, Louis Jordan, Christine Clark, Bobby Rydell, Chubby Checker, Freddie Cannon, Patti LaBelle. I like to think that our singing helped support and sell millions of successful records. When Clara had free time, I would add her to the group doing background on recordings. If you listen to Dee Dee's million-seller Cameo hit "Mashed Potatoes," you'll recognize her voice.

When the Beatles came on the scene, the action dried up for a lot of us. Many promoters and companies went out of business in 1964–65. We did only a few gigs for New York studios and for Harold B. Robinson in Philadelphia. Sweet and shy Patti LaBelle was his pet. He would put his palms against her cheeks and talk to her as if she were a kid: "Come on, Patti baby, you can do it—open up." Boy, did she ever open up! Soon after that she formed her own group.

I STILL wanted to play and sing, but since I knew John wasn't going to change his ways, I decided to do a single. Eventually, I worked the best nightclubs in New York, New Jersey, Pennsylvania, and Ohio.

When I got my first job as a single at the Twenty-One Key Club in downtown Philadelphia, a whole new world opened up for me. The hours were long but oh, so much fun. I ate dinner at the club, then worked the regular 9 P.M. to 2 A.M. club time plus one more hour past closing. The doors would be locked to newcomers then, but those already inside were provided all their "for the road" requests. I got an amazing amount of publicity too; newspapers and black radio stations were full of the story that "Willa Ward of the Famous Ward Singers" was working a nightclub. Duke Morgan, a promoter and columnist for the *Pittsburgh Courier*, did a full page on me and my new venture.

One of the people I met at the Twenty-One Key Club, a Mr. Tully of the William Morris agency, gave me another chance to work Las Vegas. He offered me three months at the Tropicana for $700 a week plus free room and food. True to form, John again forbade me to go. Had I accepted the job, it would have been another Ward first, for until that time no black female singer had been featured at the casinos. Remembering that just a few years earlier we had been denied food even from back doors and windows, I truly regretted not being the one who cracked the barrier that kept nonwhites from participating in the pleasures of the Vegas strip.

*A*FTER BOOKING agent Max Gordon came to a Ward Singers' concert in the Philadelphia Arena, he was determined to get Clara into nightclubs. She had already discussed such a step with journalist Richard Gehman but had not been sold on the proposal. Yet now, much to the surprise of many people and after much soul-searching, Clara decided to take her talent and the Gospel to the nighclub world. Booking agents who surmised that they could push my sister into singing blues and jazz, however, learned how committed she was to Gospel when she turned down an offer of $10,000 to do so. She reasoned that the secular sector needed and deserved the musical ministry she had to offer as much as churchgoing folks did.

Having accepted the challenge, Clara forged straight ahead. Her pilot appearance in New York at the Village Vanguard opened to rave reviews. My sister found that nightclub audiences could be moved to distraction. Their drinks sat waiting to be lifted by hands that were fully engaged in clapping to the spirit. Clara's misgivings were drowned in a vat of enthusiasm that the club patrons kept filled to the brim.

Mom, of course, hit the ceiling. She told Clara, "You're going to hell in a basket—just like your sister. God is going to fix you." With that prediction, Mom dropped the puppet strings for a while; it was some time before she would even come to a nightclub. But when Clara signed with Jeanette Darnell of BBS Records at $7,000 plus 60 percent of her recording revenue per year, Mom softened her stance considerably. She still didn't like club work, but she liked giving up dinero even less.

REPORTERS HAVE often asked, "When did the crossover from all-black to mixed or all-white audiences come about?" Clara once explained it this way:

> The breakthrough came little by little. A lot of white promoters thought of us in terms of black acceptance only, but a few realized the full potential of our mass appeal. I recognized it when we worked the college circuit all over the country. The kids were mostly white. They were having as good a time as blacks at a camp meeting. The universal soul bonding was happening. The places were always jammed to the rafters.
>
> I remember years ago, some white southerners would go to the churches of their workers to hear "Negro singing." Black and white often sang the same Isaac Watts hymns at church, but our interpretations and deliveries were quite different, and as Mom said, "You could hear the gap closing as the whites started adopting our style of singing." So when people ask me why I think conservative white Americans—young and old, rich or poor—flock to our shows, I like to say, "Whether they're Texas oil men or mechanics and nurses from Milwaukee or Maine, the soul responds to spiritual stimuli. There is no color involved, just feelings. Lord knows it feels good."
>
> A gospel singer cannot be successful without living and breathing every word he or she sings. Just like friends, Gospel songs cheer folks when they're downhearted, and they give people hope to continue their daily lives even when times look bleak. They can bring sweet and wonderful messages to the lonely and sick. Perhaps this explains

how we cannot turn our backs on requests from the audience. You never know just how much it might mean to the requester.

It is by no means an easy life, but it is impossible to resist the joy of bringing happiness to people—people everywhere. The body gets tired, but to me it's the most satisfying of all possible existences.

My only regret is that I haven't stopped long enough to get married again. We never spend more than a week a year at home anymore. I only had one vacation in my life as an adult. Oh well, you can't have everything.

*I*T WAS in 1962 that Clara was first booked at the New Frontier in Las Vegas. She took enough clothes for the three-week engagement—and was totally dumfounded when at the end of the first week the casino owners picked up all four options specified in her contract. As it turned out, that gig lasted five years. Thinking about it later, Clara recalled:

During the first show we did square songs [the soft songs that most white people sang], but as the night went on we started pulling out our Gospel blockbusters. Our 4 A.M. show was the one when all the mammoth stars showed up. People like Steve Allen, Edie Gormé, Dean Martin, and Sammy Davis Jr. scrambled for front-row seats. Even political biggies like Ted Kennedy, his wife, and cronies became hand-clapping supporters. They were all so warm and up. It was almost like a revival—a five-year revival. We were mighty proud.

We were told that people in Vegas don't listen to what you're doing on stage. That's not true. They listened, participated, and stood in long lines outside waiting their turn to be a part of our audience.

After all the one-nighters and traveling, it was nice to settle down a bit in Vegas and have a home atmosphere. It was the first time in ages I had a chance to do some home cooking. Every now and then, some of those celebrities would come home with me for a "Down-home breakfast"—with grits and biscuits.

Most singers would have given their eyeteeth to work Vegas on a forty-week basis for one year, let alone five, but the Clara Ward Singers did that and more. For seven years running they spent their summers working the Golden Horseshoe at Disneyland in California. "Walt Disney himself told us he loved our work so much that we had a home at Disneyland," said Clara.

Given her own schedule during those years, it might seem that Clara must often have been in two places at the same time. The explanation is that when her popularity called her away, her employers in Las Vegas graciously gave her a leave of absence to fill that engagement. While Clara was performing elsewhere, Mom would assign other singers to fill in for her.

Mom was kept busy designing the glitter gowns and outlandish hairdos that became the singers' trademark. She handsewed every gown with stitches so fine and so even that the work looked machine-made, and the coiffures took as much time and imagination as the wardrobe. Clara laughingly told me, "There were as many people asking how we kept our hair on with all our movement as there were requesting songs."

Most flamboyant of Mom's wig styles was a towering cone-shaped do with a white streak that ran like a bolt of lightning from peak to crown. Some folks called it the "skunk wig," a far cry from Mom's lofty intentions in designing it. She had adapted the shape from a bishop's miter and added the streak to symbolize being zapped by the Holy Spirit.

Wigs and hairpieces had figured in the Ward Singers' "look" since the group's early days. I remember as far back as 1940, when I was pregnant with Charlotte and Mom and Clara came to see me, they were both wearing "Page Boy" additions: straight hair descending to the shoulders and ending in a seriously tight undercurl like a long, horizontal Tootsie Roll. To me, they looked like movie stars, and I yelled,

"I've got to have one—gotta get me a Page Boy!" But John yelled right back, "Oh no, you don't. I don't want you wearing a wig, even if it's only a half one." He decided to give me a perm so I could style my own hair that way, and the next day he began by applying a lye-based straightener. Obviously, it was left on too long, for by the end of the week I too looked like a movie star—Yul Brynner. Ironically, out of necessity I ended up wearing a full wig for some time. My hair grew back, but never to its original fullness or texture.

*I*T WAS STILL 1962 when Mom called me to brag about how much money they were making and how much cash was getting away because they were too busy to accept all the offers. "Willa, you could be making some of these thousands if you had a gospel group," she kept telling me. I must say, the thought got more intriguing with each call, and I decided to pursue it.

Mom came east when I told her about my newly formed group. She said she wanted to hear us and set up an audition with a collection of promoters in New York City. With great hopes, we went with Mom to the Big Apple. Following introductions all around, my singers and I were off to the dressing room to change into our "working clothes." I knew we were in trouble the minute we came out and Mom shrieked, "Your dresses are too short, your dresses are too short!" (In fact, they were a good three inches below the knee.) The bubbles went out of us. We tried to recover and sing with enthusiasm, but from the first chorus Mom rolled her eyes skyward, shook her head, frowned, threw her hands up, and spoke with great animation to the promoters she was sitting with. At the end of the session we were told, "We'll call you." Sure!

We asked Mom why she had behaved that way and what caused the producers to dismiss us so abruptly. "You sounded awful. I told them I'd try to get you all together," is what she told us. I knew we could sing, but I didn't know until later that how we sounded had little to do with it. The fact was that Mom had two singers too many but wanted to have them where she could put her hands on them if she needed them. This is how she worked it. After my singers left in a huff and we were alone together, she told me, "The group has no excitement—you won't sell. I'll get you some singers that will knock them out." Before I could collect my wits, Mom had sent Shirley Smith from Detroit and Helen Johnson from California to my house. They slept, drank, and ate there while we rehearsed. I went to work at a posh gay club, Drury Lane, using my salary to support the group and keep them in the style they had been accustomed to.

Eventually, we began getting jobs in New York, New Jersey, and Pennsylvania. Our territory, like our recognition was expanding. My Gospel group (Helen Johnson, Shirley Smith, Madeline Thompson, my daughter Rita Moultrie, and I) was doing all right. That is, until Mom intervened again. Just as we were meshing well together, she called Madeline to say how desperately she needed her in California. Eventually the discord in our splintered group was full-blown. Helen left too and went back to California, and Shirley went home to Detroit. In short order they were both back working with Clara's group.

MEANWHILE, though, we'd had some good gigs. Le Bistro in Atlantic City was fun. For the last show of each night we donned white robes and halos, and the emcee introduced us as Willa Ward and the Belting Night Angels. We had a great time with the concept and costumes.

We were the only constants during that three-week engagement. The first week showcased singer Evelyn Simms; the second, Milt Trennier of the Trennier Brothers band. The fabulous Jack Jones also appeared at Le Bistro while we were there. Jack's singing knocked us out,

and his sincerity and warmth offstage were equally impressive. Each
night he would hurry back to his motel after the last show to be with
his wife and baby. I was shocked to learn later that he and his wife had
parted.

The club's owner, a Mr. Koker, wanted to manage us and book us
into his club in Miami Beach. But John still didn't like the thought of
someone else pulling my chain, so another good opportunity bit the
dust. Nevertheless, the word obviously got around Atlantic City that
we had a good show. One night I got a telegram at Le Bistro: "Willa,
you and the gang are invited to attend the Club Harlem famous
celebrity breakfast show 6:00 A.M. Sunday. We would be honored to
have you. Please come. Jack Southern, your host."

The honor—as for any performers who got such an invitation—was
ours. Club Harlem, on Kentucky Avenue in Atlantic City, stayed open
twenty-four hours a day. Its front bar featured swinging bands; in the
big back room, Vegas-style shows—gorgeous costumes, willowy show-
girls, headline entertainers—had would-be patrons (racially mixed but
predominantly white) lined up around the block for the five hundred
available seats.

*W*HILE MOM and Clara were working in Vegas and
California, they would sometimes fly east to do
the Steve Allen and Johnny Carson shows. I didn't
mind not being asked to join them in New York, but when they came to
Philadelphia for the Mike Douglas show, I felt bad about being ex-
cluded. I could easily have made the taping sessions, especially when I
was working at Arthur's Steak House, just a block from the studio. I even
went down there to see them rehearse, wondering if they would ask me
to join them. They never did.

Eventually, our only frictionless episodes were the occasions when we sang at civil rights rallies or fund raisers. When our King—Martin Luther—was giving his heart and soul to effect a positive change in our fractured country, we gladly did what we could to help advance the monumental cause he championed.

We had also traveled with John Kennedy and Lyndon Johnson when they were hot on the campaign trail in 1960, serving as crowd warmers before the speakers took the stage. And at a Madison Square Garden rally for LBJ in 1964, the crowd had to be calmed down after we sang. They were so fired up, it took a while before the people on the platform could make themselves heard over the din. For President Johnson's 1965 inaugural ceremonies and gala, Mom even lent me one of her mink coats so I could be dressed in finery like hers and Clara's. I sat encircled by politicians and celebrities, enjoying the pomp and circumstance and sense of history in the making.

Clara had mixed feeling about our relationship. As close as she and I had always been, there now seemed to be an undercurrent unsettling that closeness. I had no doubt she loved me, but I knew she still envied my independence and wanted so much to experience it herself. My sister eventually found a measure of that independence as the Wards' bookings became too numerous for one group to fill. Once we had our own separate groups, Clara was able for the first time to be at least partially on her own.

Homecoming concert after a
tour, 1957. Front row, left to
right: Gertrude Ward (standing
at podium), Mildred Falls
(pianist for Mahalia Jackson),
unidentified fan, Mahalia
Jackson, Theodore Frye
(songwriter and publisher).
*Photo by Carl Poindexter. All photos
from the author's collection.*

The Gay Charmers, Willa's group, 1958. Doris Gibson
(top), Della Jo Campbell (left), Willa Ward (right).
Photo by Michael Denning.

The audience of 25,000 people assembled for a Ward Singers' program at Philadelphia's Convention Hall, 1958. *Photo by Wert S. Hooper.*

Gertrude Ward with her granddaughters, Charlotte and Rita Moultrie, at the Convention Hall anniversary, 1958.

George and Gertrude Ward saying goodbye at Philadelphia International Airport, 1959. *Photo by Ruben E. Hall.*

Hoagy Carmichael and the Ward Singers on the TV special *Those Ragtime Years*, 1959. The singers, left to right: Clara, Christine Stark, Viola Crowley, Mildred Means, Willa, Gertrude. *Photo by James C. Campbell.*

The Famous Ward Singers leaving for their first European tour, 1959. Bottom to top: Edna Crockett, Clara and Gertrude Ward, Dorothy Holmes, Mildred Means, Jessie Tucker, Bobby Thompson (organist).

The Famous Ward Singers taping a Steve Allen TV show, 1959. Clara is in front. Behind her, left to right: Jessie Tucker, Mildred Means, Dorothy Holmes, Gertrude (in center), Edna Crockett, Willa, and Vermida Royster (behind microphone).

The Reverend C. L. Franklin (Aretha's father) presenting the Fisk Jubilee award to the Clara Ward Singers, 1960. Left to right: Clara, Gertrude, and Willa.

Gertrude and Clara Ward at a recording session for Dot Records, New York, 1960. *Photo by "Popsie."*

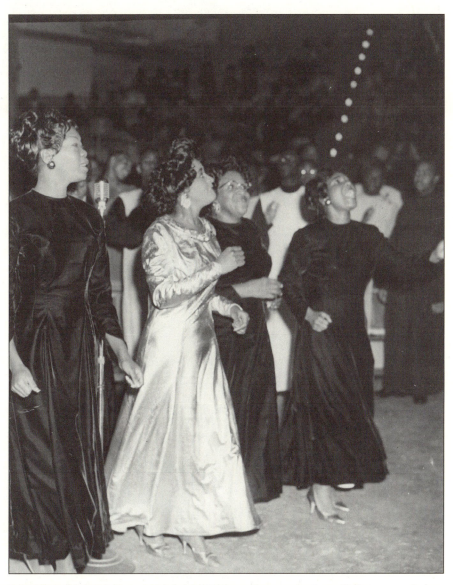

The Clara Ward Singers at the Philadelphia Met with evangelist Leroy Jenkins, 1972. Left to right: Madeline Thompson, Clara, Gertrude, Viola Crowley. *Photo by Ruben E. Hall.*

Clara Ward,
c. 1960. *Photo by
James J. Kriegsmann.*

Martin L. King Jr.,
Clara Ward, and the
Reverend William H.
Gray Sr. at a rally in
Philadelphia, 1961.

George Ward, 1962.

Gertrude Ward, 1963. *Photo by James J. Kriegsmann.*

The Gertrude Ward Singers in Japan, 1963. Left to right: Bernard Davis (at the piano), Adele Schofield, Dorothy Holmes, Gertrude Ward, Alice Houston, Helen Johnson, Bobby Thompson (at the Hammond organ).

The Gertrude Ward Singers with Gospel singer Alex Bradford in Hawaii, 1963. Left to right: unidentified fan, Gloria Berry, Bernard Davis, Alice Houston, Clara and Gertrude Ward in front of unidentified fans, Sandra Mitchell, Alex Bradford, unidentified fan.

Willa's group, then called the Willa Moultrie Singers, 1963. Left to right: seated, Rita Moultrie, Willa; standing, Helen Johnson, Madeline Thompson, Shirley Smith. *Photo by John Joseph.*

Willa's duo with Toni Rose in an Edge Supper Club ad from *Scoop* (Philadelphia), 1962.

THE NEW and BEAUTIFUL
EDGE SUPPER CLUB
695 N. Broad St.

Wila Moultrie Duo with Toni Rose on Drums
formerly (THE GAY CHARMERS)

FINEST FOOD SERVED BUFFET STYLE

added attraction
Bubbles Ross Trio
in the Lounge
for resv. call

beginning TUES.
SEPT. 13th—9pm

CE 6—3320 PO5—8812

Part Three : 1963–1981

*I*N 1963, from the pivotal point of Gospel music, Clara, Mom, and I went our three, seemingly separate ways. Actually, though, we just took different routes to the same lofty plateau, each of the Wards' accomplishments reflecting the other. As the press reported, in essence, "The Wards are singing everywhere." Clara was on Broadway, I was at Radio City Music Hall, and Mom was touring in Japan.

Clara was starring as Birdie Lee in *Tambourines to Glory*, a play by Langston Hughes (adapted from his novel) with music by Jobe Huntley. She had played the role some years earlier in summer stock. Now, at the Little Theatre in New York under the direction of Nikos Psacharopoulous, the show's cast of veteran actors included Hilda Simms (best known for some two thousand performances in the title role of *Anna Lucasta*), Rosetta Le Noire (with Broadway credits ranging from Pitti Sing in *The Hot Mikado* to Bloody Mary in *South Pacific*), Lou Gossett Jr. (whose prominence as a stage and screen actor has only increased since then), Robert Guillaume (on- and off-Broadway actor and singer, perhaps now most familiar from TV's *Benson*), Brother John Sellers (who traveled and performed extensively with Mahalia Jackson), Micki Grant (herself a poet, playwright, and songwriter), Anna English (nightclub singer and dancer as well as stage performer), and Joseph Attles (whose roles included Sportin' Life in a European tour of *Porgy and Bess*).

*T*HE EASTMAN Boomer theatrical agency had offered Clara $7,000 a week to headline the first Gospel theme show at Radio City Music Hall in New York City. As wonderful as the proposal was, given her other commitments she had to turn it down. Not having anticipated any problem with signing the Clara Ward Singers, the programming director had already started work on a show based on a Gospel group's performance. Clara suggested my singers.

Mr. Boomer called me a few days later to report that the Music Hall people would be auditioning Gospel groups and suggested that we come to the tryouts. Rita Moultrie (my daughter), Madeline Thompson, Shirley Smith, Helen Johnson, and I—then known as the Willa Moultrie Singers—went to New York, expecting to compete with just a few groups, but to our surprise they numbered thirty! We heard some wonderful voices stretching to their limits, and with each performance our own hopes dwindled. The producers praised my arrangements, but they wanted to find out how we performed before a live audience. So Bernie Rothbard got us a job at a folk house in Jersey called the Barn, and the New Yorkers came down to see us. We turned the house out.

Still, I was stunned when manager Marc Platt informed me that we had been chosen to work Radio City Music Hall's magnificent stage. We did four shows a day, seven days a week, to six thousand people a show and were received so well that we were held over for another four weeks. Fateful timing may have gotten us there in the first place, but we worked hard to make them ask us back—and they did, twice. In 1967 and 1969 the Willa Ward Singers—Arlene Mills, Evelyn Vinson, Esther Ford, Gloria Berry, and Rita Palmer, together with my daughter Rita Moultrie Bell and me—appeared there again, the only Gospel group ever to do so.

The Music Hall, the world's largest theater, is a full city block wide and has a sixty-foot-high proscenium arch. When the curtain opened on our 1967 performance, we stood on a tall black pyramid flanked by

our drummer Sticks Evans and organist Bobby Banks. I began with
"Sometimes I Feel like a Motherless Child," followed by Rita singing
"Down by the Riverside." The movie screen behind us suddenly became
brilliant with images of leaping flames, and smoke whiffed up from the
front of the stage. Then, as Esther Ford soloed on "Swing Low, Sweet
Chariot," the overhead area was bathed in golden light to complete the
effect of Heaven and Hell both pulling for newcomers. In a spectacular
finale the sixty-piece orchestra was joined by the hall's grand organ, and
the Rockettes and a full ballet troupe performed as I led my singers in a
rousing rendition of "When the Saints Go Marching In." The audience
was left in no doubt which way we were headed: our lifts rose and we
slowly ascended to the clouds.

The press loved it, and we loved the reviews, including one by
George Levitan in the magazine *Sepia:*

WILLA WARD SINGERS AT RADIO CITY MUSIC HALL AGAIN

The fabulous Willa Ward, who comes from a family long associated
with the tops in gospel singing, is more than up to the challenge of
working the great Hall. She is as lovely as ever, and as talented as always. The Willa Ward Singers have returned to Radio City in New
York City after repeated requests from admirers.

Back in 1963 the Willa Ward Singers packed them in at Radio
City. They were the first gospel singers to appear on showtown's
biggest most elaborate stage. And now they're back for another 6
week stand. . . .

Willa's mother, Gertrude Ward, formed the famous Ward
Singers, which included Willa and her sister Clara. Mama Ward was
a strict teacher, as well as a proud mother. When Clara formed her
own group, Mama traveled with the Clara Ward Singers to offer bits
of advice and lots of moral support. . . .

When Willa got the idea to start a gospel group of her own, she
had been doing pop music shows in nightclubs, mixing in a good portion of that gospel flavor, and when gospel singing had a revival, Willa
had one too. [Winning the Hall's auditions in 1963 is] proof of how
well she selected the talent and songs and wrote the arrangements.

ON ONE occasion, when Clara and I had an evening off from our respective shows, we decided to visit some clubs and personalities also working in New York. Our first stop was at a downtown club whose headliner was the inimitable Hildegarde, then at the top of her popularity. We were never shown to a table but stood at the back of the room for a half-hour or so enjoying her easy, entertaining style. As we edged toward the exit, Hildegarde called out, "Good night, ladies" and gave us the OK sign. We had never met her, but one entertainer often recognizes another and salutes a kindred soul. It was interesting to see all the other white faces turn toward us, staring in puzzlement. We smiled and waved goodbye to the gracious lady on stage.

From there we went to the Café Ambassador located in the Sheraton East on Park Avenue. You might imagine that the host would have enough class at least to make polite excuses as to why we weren't escorted to seats, as were others who came in after we did. Instead, he just ignored us. After a humiliating stretch of time, I said to Clara, "I'm going to ask him why we are being treated in this fashion." She whispered, "You know why; just wait a little longer." When I approached him, he smiled a face-stretching smile without warmth and asked politely, "May I help you?" "Yes, you may," I told him. "We came to hear Bobby Short." More waiting. Finally, he offered, "I'm sorry, but in order to be seated, women must be escorted by a male who has made a reservation." As we turned to go, a man who had just come out of the room asked, "Aren't you Miss Ward? My wife and I saw you last week in the Langston Hughes play." Clara smiled and asked if they had enjoyed it. He said they had, and then he turned to the host: "My wife and I would like these people to be our guests at our table." As we strutted in, it was easy to see from the host's expression that the turn of events was not to his liking. We were delighted, of course, and thanks to those kind people whose table was shared, we got to see and hear Bobby Short after all.

MOM HERSELF had put together the Gertrude Ward Singers, a group with unusual flair. Because of the loss of her own singing voice, she was limited to evangelism and strutting, but Gert had a special talent for intertwining various elements of vocal communication and body language. The whole package was quite effective.

As Clara and I were doing our separate things in New York City, Mom was wowing them in Japan. The people there had never been exposed to a Momma like my Momma. The usually reserved folks of that country, I'm told, were soon yelling and applauding wildly; some were even dancing in the aisles.

When Mom returned home, though, she was upset that my group had done so well at Radio City Music Hall. She had said that my group could never work the same jobs as Clara's because we didn't measure up. She was concerned that "people might get us mixed up and assume Clara's group was slipping." So now she called Marc Platt and told him that given enough notice, the Clara Ward Singers would be available to appear at Radio City. Imagine her anger when Mr. Platt replied, "I thank you for your call, but everyone here is just wild about Willa's group."

Clara relayed that conversation to me and said, "Willa, you're gonna get it now!" Reluctant to upset her by putting her in the middle, I didn't tell Clara that I'd already "gotten it" from Mom. I'd had to move the telephone receiver away from my ear because her voice had that piercing "I'm mad as hell" sound. "Well, you're a fine one," she screeched. "You knew that was our job. You should have told him you weren't interested in working the hall again. Well, that's the last time you'll do that. I won't put another thing your way—ever!"

She even called Mr. Boomer, threatening to leave his agency if they booked my group again. And to teach me a lesson, Mom made a point of bringing Clara east to take jobs that might otherwise have gone to my group. I had to keep quiet about our continuing affiliation with the Eastman Boomer agency and others.

*W*HEN I had a goiter operation, Mom visited me every day at the hospital. My doctor told me to avoid all speech, as talking could and probably would impair my voice permanently. My husband had brought a chalk- board so that I could write anything I wished to convey. But Mom said, "Willa, you can talk if you want to. God has healed me." I don't know why she thought or said that. When she had the same operation, she ignored her doctor's advice not to talk, and her voice was never the same again.

Mom had always preached, though, that Dr. Jesus would take care of all ills. If something didn't heal or work out, she said, "It's His plan— it's the Master's will." When Dorothy Holmes, one of her singers, got sick on the road and wanted professional medical help, Mom talked her out of getting it. Dorothy died, and her family threatened to sue unless Mom agreed to pick up the full expense of shipping the body home and to pay for all the funeral arrangements.

My father went with John and me to our daughter Charlotte's grad- uation from Hampton Institute in Virginia. Sitting in the auditorium, Daddy was experiencing back and side pains. We all attributed them to the long car ride, but the pain persisted and, on the way home, shifted to his left side. Back in Philadelphia I tried to persuade him to see a doc- tor, but he too was sure that rest and prayer would make everything all right. The next time I spoke with him he assured me that he was feeling much better, so I stopped asking.

I was totally unprepared when my husband called me at the club where I was working to say my father had had a heart attack. I went to Temple University Hospital that night but wasn't allowed to see him. The next morning I took Daddy's robe and toiletries to his room. He was hooked up to various hospital equipment and looked weak, but he was quite lucid. When I asked why he hadn't called me when he felt bad, his response was, "You got your own house and family to look out for. I'll make it okay."

I phoned Mom in California to give her the news and was told, "If Daddy is not worse, then he must be getting better, so I'll finish the engagement out and then come." My father in fact did respond well to hospital treatment, then signed himself out. Mom still had not come home.

My Uncle David—Mom's brother from South Carolina—was then living in the basement apartment of my parents' house, but they saw each other infrequently. Daddy went his way, and Uncle David didn't venture out of his quarters very often. His diabetes was uncontrolled because he didn't have the money to pay for the medication he needed, at least not enough to stabilize his condition. I started checking on Daddy and Uncle David more often than before.

Daddy was talking less and less. I think by then his morale was at an all-time low, his will chiseled away by the difficulties of his life. Yet as caustic-tongued and unyielding as Mom was, he missed her and us very much. My uncles J.P. and Charlie had died not long before, increasing his awareness of his own inevitable mortality.

To add to my father's state of despair, Uncle David got worse and had to be hospitalized, leaving Daddy totally alone in the house. Aunt Clara and I took my uncle to Temple University Hospital, where he died three weeks later. When Mom came home to make funeral arrangements, my father had just left the hospital for the second time himself and was in no condition to be going over papers and taking care of other details.

Going to their house, I found Mom on the phone and Daddy slouched in a chair. About all I could do was write some cards to relatives—giving details of Uncle David's demise—and make coffee. I was ready to leave when I got such a strong desire to embrace my father that I turned and did just that. I hugged him, kissed his forehead, and smiled a goodbye. Two hours later Mom was on the phone shouting, "I think Daddy's dead!" We rushed through the rain, to find the rescue squad already there and trying to revive him. But George Ward—father and husband of the original World-Famous Ward Singers—was gone.

There was a double service at Mutchmore Memorial Baptist Church,

Uncle David on one side of the pulpit and my father on the other, lying at peace in their twin coffins. Daddy was buried in Philadelphia, but Uncle David's body was shipped to South Carolina. We all went down to the final services for him at old Ebenezer Church.

*E*VEN THOUGH we'd spent most of our lives going here and there, Clara and I had had enough time with our father to afford us a strong, loving bond. As happens very often, that bond tightened and grew even more loving after death.

I felt much the same about our Aunt Clara, who all during the lean years had bent over backward to aid us in any way she could. Some of my fondest childhood memories are still of eating her food, sleeping in her beds, sheltered by her roof and her loving-kindness. She was crushed at being snubbed by Mom when times got better for us, and Aunt Clara was declared too worldly, too sinful to associate with.

I secretly visited Aunt Clara whenever I could, sometimes with a few dollars or candy or fruit. She kept all the cards and notes I sent when I was on the road, and they served to evoke endless questions and inquiries about my travels. She gleefully consumed each detail and description until she had it down pat. She would ask me to tell the stories over and over again and correct me if I left out the smallest detail. She was fun to be with.

When death came to Aunt Clara in 1977, everyone was surprised that all her worldly goods and assets were left to me—except for $500 that I was to give to Acey. Each installment was paid to him on the porch, for I felt uncomfortable about allowing him to enter my home and space.

Y THE mid-1960s Clara was very popular in Europe. In December 1965 she and the group were enjoying a marvelous run in London clubs and on BBC television, constantly swamped by photographers and reporters as they moved from place to place.

From London, their travels took them to Paris and its Olympia Theatre, where they were booked for five weeks, which was three weeks longer than any other group or single had ever worked there. A Paris newspaper correctly stated, "All of a sudden Europeans, especially young Parisians, have been bitten by the gospel bug. Let's face it, we have liked American Negro Music for a long, long time. It used to be hard jazz. Now it's gospel! I think it's because this music gives us even more of a strong beat and a helluva lot more soul than we get from even the best of those jazz fellows. Gospel song records are on sale everywhere."

Mom had flown to London and then on to Paris with Clara. Our friend Gladys Bonds joined them in Paris, and from there she and Mom embarked on a pilgrimage to the Holy Land for Christmas. Clara spent Christmas in her hotel room, alone but not lonely. The hotel staff decorated a lovely tree in her bedroom while Clara was at dinner, and New Year's Day her suite was full of gifts and cards from loyal fans and friends all over the world.

In the meantime, Mom was being showered with attention on her sojourn. Her full-length mink coat prompted the locals to call her the "Black Queen Mother"; it seems they had seen the queen of England in a similar fur. Mrs. Bonds said Mom really milked the royalty bit. Clara had gotten so much publicity on her Holy Land trip that Mom was not about to be outdone, but I'm sure she wanted to visit the sites for religious reasons as well. In spite of her eccentricities, Mom's faith and devotion were sure and true.

Mom and Mrs. Bonds came back via Paris, where one of the press people asked, "What do you have to say when people object to your singing in places like nightclubs and Disneyland?" Mom's change of heart was clear in her answer:

> I don't know if they've accepted it by now or not. They thought that when we went out into the clubs, we'd be singing blues and jazz or even rock-and-roll, but we sing the same songs in the clubs that we sing in church. It's wonderful how they accept Gospel singing, sometimes even more than people in the church.
>
> I remember when we were in Oslo, Norway, in a club where everybody was drinking, and most had never heard of the Ward Singers. But as we began our first song, we saw people taking their glasses off the tables and putting them on the floor next to their chairs. When we finished, there was not a glass on any table in the whole place. Everyone was strictly listening to the music and clapping their hands. You'd have thought you were in a sanctified church. It's been that way everywhere we've gone in the world. And when it comes to foul language, I've heard worse in some churches and from the mouths of the "holy" than I've ever heard in any nightclub. We've sung in Las Vegas for years, four times a night, and have never once heard foul language.
>
> The Bible says, and Christ told His disciples, "Go ye into all the world and preach the Gospel to every creature. He that believeth shall be saved, but he that believeth not shall be damned" [Mark 16:15–16]. And He didn't stop there. A little farther on, in Luke [14:23], He said, "Go out into the highways and hedges and compel them to come in, that my·house shall be filled." I believe we have reached out and touched as many souls in the nightclubs as we have in churches.
>
> People say we look like clowns in our gowns and wild hairdos. Can you imagine someone who is supposed to be a Christian concentrating on how we look rather than how many people we make conscious of the Lord's presence? These same backstabbers are usually the ones doing everything in the book of sin through the week and picking up the Holy Bible and shouting on Sunday. A bum with the purest heart is not welcome in the church, because he doesn't dress and smell right.

We have got to rethink what is important and what's not. Nobody says anything of the Pope in his elaborate gold-embroidered robes or the bishops' fancy mitered hats. African tribal leaders were heavily adorned in their own styles of finery. The medicine men also wore special and different dress. It's just what you get used to seeing. The Lord didn't make or design any religious outfits. People designed them to be spectacular and out of the ordinary, something apart from regular attire. We aren't bishops or tribal leaders, but we are messengers and our "special look" rings the bell so we can get into your souls. Amen!

Clara added, "When we sing you can call it a religious service or a concert—it can be both. The audience is sometimes a religious group, and if they're not, they get a good feeling anyway—and that may be the start of an active relationship with the Holy Spirit. If a person feels uplifted after seeing and hearing us sing the Gospel, it doesn't matter what they think it is; the truth is that it's a plus, a positive, anyway you look at it. None of us in the group ever won a beauty contest, but our work is not about that. After we make a first impression, we enter something else into the system: the words of the Gospel. Our mission, our purpose, is to help mesh the mind, spirit, and soul into a sweeter, more loving partnership, to introduce the beauty of our Lord!"

*L*OVE ON the road—Mom probably didn't want to know about it, but of course it happened.

For a brief period, Clara and Roberto Clemente, right fielder for the Pittsburgh Pirates, were tight. Clara joked that the stereotype of the ardent Latin lover was exaggerated in this instance, given poor Roberto's bad back. Their sessions usually ended with Clara massaging the full length of Rob's aching spine.

They also spent hours discussing the injustices perpetrated against minorities. Roberto opened his heart to Clara, telling her of his deep hurt at not having his acceptance equal his exceptional talent and repeated contributions to the game of baseball. That this pussycat who often came on like a tiger had concerns beyond his stellar career and his private problems, however, was shown by his tragic death in a plane crash while on a hunger mission to Latin America.

Others in the group had celebrity lovers—a trumpeter, a crooner, a screen star who would send his chauffeur to pick up his selected Ward singer. Well, I guess "everybody loves somebody sometime."

*I*N 1966 our guys in Vietnam were being demoralized by confusion of purpose and the negative and dissenting voices stateside. A lot of soldiers interviewed near the battle line lacked the convictions of dedicated warriors. I would venture to say that the absence of spirit may have dulled their edge and increased their vulnerability to injury or death.

All the boys were subject to this malaise—black and white. Yet as James Baccon lamented in the *Hollywood Reporter,*

> Big-name Negro entertainers aren't trekking to Vietnam. [According to] George Chandler, head of the [U.S.O. Overseas] Committee, the boys over there, especially the Negro G.I.'s, keep asking for Harry Belafonte, the Sammy Davises, the Sidney Poitiers, and the Bill Cosbys. I contacted their agents repeatedly, but it's a strange situation. I get so little response. . . .
>
> Good or bad, win or lose, the cause and effect of this war is totally apart from trying to supply our lads away from home with that which they so desperately need, uplifting support!

Clara agreed wholeheartedly. Disturbed when she learned how few black performers—whatever their reasons—were making the trip to the

Far East where our American sons, fathers, and brothers were putting their lives on the line, she made an immediate decision to go. "Until a few weeks ago, she said, "I never realized how desperately performers were needed over there. I feel the Ward Singers can help give them a touch of home, as our music is of a religious nature! I'm sure our special treatment of their favorite hymns and Gospel songs will help lift their spirits. We're gonna give our all 'cause that's what they're doing." She was one of what Chandler called "people who saw the great need, like John Bubbles, Pearl Bailey, and the wonderful Clara Ward."

Clara canceled five weeks of engagements in order to accept the invitations of the Department of State and the USO (United Service Organization) to visit Vietnam for three weeks. She and Mildred Means, Mavilyn Simpson, Madeline Thompson, and accompanist Alton Williams left on November 14, 1966, for a tour that covered military bases, hospitals, remote campsites, and destroyers. They performed at officers' clubs, service clubs, on radio and television, and even at the Koza Baptist Church in Okinawa. "Once we got settled in our first base quarters," Clara reported later, "we were ready to go. We did two shows a day to incredibly enthusiastic audiences. I'll never forget any of it, but the men on the destroyer *Corpus Christi* in Camranh Bay, Vietnam, made leaving them difficult. They were fantastic."

Before Clara went overseas, she had been having such severe headaches that her doctor advised her not to go; under the stress of war, he feared, her already elevated blood pressure might soar even higher. But my sister's commitment to our guys in the Far East took precedence over her personal concern. In fact, Clara said, all her headaches went away and all her pain fled when she was presented with an appreciation award by General W. C. Westmoreland for services rendered to our fighting forces overseas.

Listening to the praise showered on her and the group, she told the press afterward, her mind took her back to the Far East:

> The morale among the men was so very great. It made me happy to
> be able to lift their spirits. The ratio of Negro to white GIs was about

1 to 4, 25 percent. What I saw was 100 percent appreciation from a group of American guys united in a common cause.

Everyone was trying to keep us from feeling panicky. If we heard any disturbing noises, they'd say, "Don't worry, that's just the practice range being used." It wasn't until we got ready to leave that they finally told us, after we had been sitting around waiting for several hours, that the airport had been bombed so nothing could go out that day. We went back to our hotel. One U.S.-occupied building right down the street had been bombed also. They had thrown a bomb into our hotel lobby but it failed to go off. Thank God. The next day we were glad to go, but more glad to have spent those three weeks with our boys. . . .

I forgot to add, we were happy and surprised to see servicewomen also doing their part. Nobody ever mentions them. It's as if they are taken for granted.

Clara also received letters of appreciation from the Hollywood Overseas Committee of the USO and the Department of the Army, and a "certificate of esteem" from the Defense Department.

CLARA HAD asked me and my daughter Rita if we wanted to go to Vietnam with them. Rita, not keen about being in a war zone, declined. The idea scared me, too, but I would have gone if my husband hadn't been sick.

I am so glad I didn't go, because I would have been away from John when he died. He and his doctor had conferred on the gravity of his illness, but neither confided in me. On his deathbed he said he had wanted to spare me the agony of knowing his death was imminent. He also told me to ask Mom "to try and give him a loving thought in death," as she'd never made him feel that "she cared for him alive." Tearfully, he said, "I loved her like a mother." Mom never forgave him for giving me my independence from her.

When Clara learned about John's death, she cried and cried for him and for me. She was worried that after twenty-six years of being taken care of, I would find survival difficult. Mom said, "I'm sorry he's dead, but you reap what you sow. God don't like ugly." I asked her what she meant by that statement—she never answered.

EVERY NOOK and cranny in my house reminded me of John. I could hardly stand it, so when Clara asked me early in 1967 if I wanted to open with them at the Castaways in Miami Beach, I jumped at the chance. I desperately needed to be with family, and I also needed money to pay for John's burial and take care of the many bills that had mounted during his illness. All our savings had been depleted.

I remember that years earlier, when we first went to Miami to sing at a black church, our aim had been to see beautiful Miami Beach. The idea was dashed when we were told that only black workers were welcome, and they had to leave at sundown. We went to the bridge connecting Miami and Miami Beach and just looked over and imagined.

This time, Clara and I checked the Beach for a place to stay, but everything not filled up was too expensive. We finally wound up at the Sir John Motel in Miami. It was in fair shape but located in what had become a dismal slum area. It had once been a beautiful hotel, frequented by the best of people. What a change it had suffered.

We had a studio apartment with a small kitchen, so I went out to stock our refrigerator with food from a nearby grocery store. On my way back, I looked up at our unit and saw little Clara standing at the window looking so pitiful and forlorn. When I got back inside, she said,

"I hate this place. I'm going to sleep until it's time to go to work." Slumber, as well as alcohol, was now her panacea. But Clara had forgotten we weren't to open until the next night, so we had a free evening. Our debate about what to do with it was solved when we learned that Billy Daniels—a pop singer sometimes billed as "the sexiest voice this side of Paradise"—was working the Beach.

Gladys Bonds and Mom arrived in town about four hours after we did. Mom was exhausted, but Mrs. Bonds was raring to go and came along with Clara and me to catch Billy's show. As usual, Sweet William had the ladies spellbound. We all went up to his suite after the show and partied hard.

The next evening we opened at the Wreck Bar, which was the big room at the Castaways. Clara's head was splitting and she was exhausted. The only time she seemed to relax and forget her pain was when she was listening to Rodney Dangerfield, who opened the show for us. (He was and still is the funniest comedian I know.) The second night, while Clara was singing "When the Storms of Life Are Raging, Stand by Me," she just slumped to the floor and lay motionless, her eyes first staring blankly and then rolling all around. I screamed, "Get a doctor, get a doctor, my sister is going to die."

We were told at the hospital that Clara had a severe aneurysm and stroke, and the prognosis was not hopeful. The doctors and nurses were preparing my sister for a spinal when she cried out, "Mom, you're the cause of me being here, you did this to me." All the years of tyranny had taken their toll, for Mom had kept Clara under constant pressure. She had to sing even when her butt was dragging. What's more, Mom kept calling agents all over the country for new singers. She would get angry and fire people almost every month and then replace them with her latest finds. The phone bills usually ran about $900 a month. That was a load in itself; even worse was the constant strain on my sister of having to train new people.

Now, after Clara's outburst, Mom started to chant and pray in a loud voice; she was really yelling. The doctor put us out of the room, but that didn't stop her. She shouted the whole night through, while I cried.

The Reverend C. L. Franklin came to the hospital to see Clara. I expected to hear him praying over her; instead he held her in his arms and talked love. "I love you, baby girl, you got to get up from that bed. You know we've got a lot of love to make and a lot of places to see and enjoy." He had stripped himself of roles and titles. He was just a man baring his emotions and begging his lady to live for love. It was very touching. At C.L.'s request, Aretha recorded "I Just Wish I Didn't Love You So"—just for Clara.

We finished out the two weeks at the Castaways without Clara. She was really missed. From there we went up to Boston to fill another engagement. At one hotel where we tried to register, the manager refused us, saying the last Gospel singers who stayed there had carried on so that the other guests were very much bothered. We don't know who they were, but we suffered the consequences of their behavior.

Two and a half weeks after Clara's collapse, she was up and dismissed from the hospital. The doctors were dumfounded; they had never seen such a recovery. They told Mom, "This is one for the books."

*W*HEN CLARA got off the plane in Philadelphia, I could see she was tiring from all the picture poses requested and questions asked by the throngs of press people. That evening the phone rang constantly with questions and concerns from all kinds of folks. The next morning's newspaper headlines read "Miracle Singer Returns Home—Healed." She may have been healed, but Clara was still weak. I took her to Dr. Holloway three times a week to make sure everything was all right. He told us that Clara must never sing hard again, but when I repeated this to Mom, her response was, "That man don't know what he's talking about. The Lord don't do no halfway healing. He saved her so she could sing Gospel."

And sing she did! Clara opened at Caesar's Palace that April (1967).

Las Vegas was teeming with talent. Phil Harris and the Kim Sisters were
at the Desert Inn. Comedian Buddy Hackett and singer Julius LaRosa
were at the Flamingo. Harry James and his orchestra and Kay Starr were
at the Fremont. Celebrities from far and near jammed Nero's Nook at
Caesar's every night to see the Clara Ward Singers. Wonderful George
Burns was there to cheer the group on; he told his old buddy Jack Benny
how good the Clara Ward Singers were, and Mr. Benny came to hear for
himself. That same night he wrote up a contract for the group to work
with him on a show that he took to Broadway for six weeks. Together,
they tore the New York audiences up every night. "Fabulous," said the
New York Daily News; "Splendid," wrote Walter Kerr in the *New York
Herald-Tribune.* The *New York Times* called the Clara Ward Singers "magnificent" and their music "hauntingly blue and bouncingly joyous."

Singer, dancer, and screen star Mitzi Gaynor wasn't one to turn
down a successful idea; she too booked Clara's group to work a tour
with her. Television hosts everywhere wanted Clara to appear on their
shows. And when newspeople asked some of the greats to put what
they thought of the Clara Ward Singers into a few words, here is what
these performers said:

ED SULLIVAN: "This you have to hear."
JACK BENNY: "I put my violin away and just listened."
GEORGE BURNS: "Just great."
DINAH SHORE: "Love them."
CAROL CHANNING: "My favorite group."
JOEY BISHOP: "They are the most."
DEAN MARTIN: "The very best—anywhere."

In addition, an informal poll conducted among West Coast theatrical
writers in Vegas named Clara Ward the best-dressed religious singer in
the world.

Clara, in turn, took out a full-page ad in a Vegas newspaper to thank
the Caesar's Palace management for being so wonderfully accommo-
dating and for making her singers' stay so pleasant.

*T*HAT YEAR, 1967, was a phenomenal one for Clara and the singers. Verve Records was happy to announce that sales of *The Faith, the Heart, the Soul of Clara Ward* were spiraling and that it had been chosen Cash Box album of the week after only two weeks of exposure.

Then there was the Monterey Jazz Festival, September 15, 16, and 17—the tenth annual gathering of stars and stargazers. The lineup of guest artists was awesome: Louis Bellson, Dizzy Gillespie, Illinois Jacquet, Don Ellis Orchestra, B. B. King, T-Bone Walker, the Clara Ward Singers, Janis Joplin, Woody Herman, Mel Tormé, the Modern Jazz Quartet, Laurinda Almeida, Gabor Szabo Quintet, Carmen McRae, Earl "Fatha" Hines, Buddy Johnson, and many more.

Mom wasn't one to leave a stone unturned when it meant advancing an idea or project; she milked the "Miracle Girl" theme to a fare-thee-well. Every time she could throw the phrase in to boost ticket sales, she did. So, a month after Monterey and ten months after that horrible evening at the Castaways in Miami, when Mom booked the group at the Academy of Music in Philadelphia, this is how the ad for that concert read:

CLARA WARD

INTERNATIONAL STAR OF BROADWAY, TELEVISION, MOVIES, AND RADIO—WITH SYMPHONY ORCHESTRA IN CONCERT AT "ACADEMY OF MUSIC"—MONDAY, OCTOBER 23, AT 8 P.M., ASSISTED BY THE FAMOUS WARD SINGERS WITH MADAM GERTRUDE WARD, MGR., AND BRINGING TO PHILADELPHIA FOR THE FIRST TIME THE 100 VOICES OF THE GOLDEN VOICES ENSEMBLE. THIS CHOIR IS HEARD ON CLARA WARD'S LATEST ALBUM ENTITLED *THE HEART, THE FAITH, THE SOUL OF CLARA WARD*, SINGING "MY MOTHER'S EYES," "AMERICA THE BEAUTIFUL," "WITHOUT A SONG," AND MANY OTHERS. THIS WILL BE CLARA'S FIRST FULL CONCERT SINCE SHE WAS MIRACULOUSLY HEALED BY GOD FROM A STROKE OF THE BRAIN. ADMISSION PRICES ARE $2.50, $3.50, $4.00, AND $5.00.

Jerry Gaghan, reporter for the *Philadelphia Daily News*, pushed the concert almost as hard:

> Clara Ward will rack up another first October 23, 1967, when she becomes the first Gospel Singer with full orchestra and chorus to be heard at the Academy of Music. Mahalia Jackson gave a recital at the Academy with piano accompanist, but Miss Ward will have a company of 100. Firsts are no novelty with the Philadelphia singer who was first Gospeler to play a jazz festival, Newport in '57 and Monterey, California, this year. She also took Gospel singing into cafés, carrying the swinging message of her spirituals to the fleshpots of Las Vegas. . . .
>
> Miss Ward has taken her gospel singing to every corner of the world and will leave for . . . Australia immediately after her Academy concert.

Well, not quite immediately, but when Clara did get to Australia, her two-week engagement lasted six. The tour was excitingly punctuated by a spot Clara did in a musical being filmed in California on the Metro lot: she sang her own original song "Soon One Morning." *A Time to Sing* was a Sam Katzman MGM production directed by Arthur Dreifuss and starring Shelley Fabares, Ed Begley, and Hank Williams Jr. Clara spent thirty-eight hours in the air, jetting to California for the filming and then back to Australia.

It was also in Australia that Clara made a live recording at a church program, beginning with the pastor's introduction and then her rendition of "How I Got Over." You can hear the excitement in the song and the listeners' response. My sister went on to share the harrowing details of the stroke that had incapacitated her and then of her miraculous healing—a testimony to the power of God and prayer. She followed with the Lord's Prayer. And then, disregarding her doctor's orders, she shouted out "When the Saints Go Marching In."

So much for never singing "hard" again.

ESTHER FORD, who worked with both the Famous Ward Singers and the Willa Ward Singers, gave a party in 1967 at which I met Harry Royster. John had been gone long enough for me to be extremely lonely and not long enough for my need of sexual activity to mellow out. Now that I reflect, I was ripe for plucking.

Although Harry and I became romantically involved, my time and commitments were still my own, so when Mom called from California asking me if I wanted to go to Japan with her and Clara, I was pleased and eager to do it. All the songs in the Ward Singers' repertoire were indelibly fixed in my brain, as I had been singing them all my life and had helped write and arrange many of them. My passport was current, and I had a lot of gowns that matched theirs. I informed my booking agent about the trip and told him not to contract anything for me that would conflict with the trip.

Three weeks before their departure date Mom called again, this time to tell me the tour was off—for me; she had gotten a replacement. Thoroughly shocked and disgusted, I kept asking, "Why did you, how could you?" Mom answered quite matter-of-factly, "Clara told me you didn't want to go. She said you would back out at the last moment because you would not leave Harry." Clara later assured me she had said no such thing. Those were Mom's sentiments.

After they came back, Mom called again to say she was coming east just to see me. This I doubted—and I was right. Mr. Boomer had casually mentioned to her that he wanted to book me into a fancy Philadelphia coffeehouse for a sizable amount of money—with the predictable result that Mom brought her group east to work the job. I wasn't even going to go hear them, but I thought if I showed up Mom might have a pang of guilt and change her vindictive ways. Not a chance. I got there while the singers were on stage. At the set's end I got up, intending to visit with them, but Mom stopped me; the girls couldn't come out between sets, she said, and the management didn't want anybody backstage. We exchanged a few sentences and that was it. I left before they came back on.

AFTER DADDY died and the work was concentrated chiefly on the West Coast, Mom and Clara eventually moved out there. They first rented an apartment and graduated to a lovely house in prestigious Baldwin Hills in Los Angeles.

Clara called me one day collect (so it wouldn't show on her bill) pouring her heart out in tale and tears. Between sobs, she said, "Will, I don't know what I'm gonna do. Mom insists on my singing every night at church. I've got to sing and sing until she thinks enough people have shouted. My head feels like it's splitting open." I asked, "Have you been to see a doctor?" "No," she said, "Mom won't let me go. She says God will take care of it. I've got a nurse that sneaks me out to her station wagon to take my pressure so Mom won't know. It's been way, way up for a while." I told her, "Don't work when you're feeling bad that way, just stay home." Clara said, "I can't. When I don't do what she wants me to, she beats me with a broom handle." I begged Clara to come back to Philadelphia and stay with me. She sounded so pitiful when she told me, "I can't, Will. I just can't, even though she's killing me. I can't leave her; I think her mind is going again, and I think I'm the only thing that's keeping her from slipping all the way." I pleaded with her to see a doctor secretly, and she said, "I'll try, Willa—I'll try."

Clara had lived under duress for so many years, her will was completely broken. Any time the phone rang and Clara picked it up, Mom would listen in. If she didn't like what was being said, Mom would curse the caller out and make Clara hang up. Clara was so afraid of having bad luck, she wouldn't think of disobeying. Her fear of the Gertrude Ward wrath kept her locked into the ever-tightening circle of which Mom was the only ringmaster.

Clara's "Goodbye, Will" sounded as if she was slowly sliding down the wall of a well; her voice just seemed to drown in her despair. After we hung up, I remembered a letter she had written me from Australia that shed some light on the stress that plagued her:

Dear Willa,

I'm so upset I just had to write you. Mom called me last night to tell me she had brought me a new spread. I don't know why she does those things. She's always buying and buying, anything she sees. I work so hard to keep things going even when I think I'm going to break. My [plane] ticket expired and I didn't tell anybody because I wanted to stay and make the money to pay all the bills she piles up.

I would have been content to stay in the apartment, but no, she had to have a big house with all new stuff. Now she had nothing better to do then go messing around in my bedroom with a new stupid bedspread. I wish I could go sit up in a tree with the Koala bears and never come down until I fell out of the tree dead. Here is an idea of the bills I pay monthly.

House	275.00	Burglar alarm	30.00
3229 Oxford (Phila.)	70.00	Mom's bedroom	112.00
Elec. - Gas	50.00	Lease car	249.00
3800 N. 18th (Phila.)	142.00	3 Color TV	150.00
Gardener	30.00	Public Finance	175.00
L Room Furn.	100.00	Household Finance	95.00
Din. Rm. Furn.	48.00	Aftra Loan	69.00
Clara Bed Rm.	115.00	Telephone	600.00
Valiant Finance	78.00		

That comes to $2,388 or more a month and I haven't added food buying and cleaning clothes, cosmetics, soaps and detergents, etc.

The damn bad part is that Mom won't even let me enjoy the place. You can't smoke or sit on the living room chairs. She won't even let me cook fish saying it will stink up the house. If I don't go crazy first, I'll see you when I get back stateside.

Clara might really have gone crazy had she known then the extent to which her debts would soon expand. My mother had always wanted a church of her own, especially after Pastor Samuel L. Spears of Ebenezer Baptist Church had ordained her as an evangelist in 1964. One time she rented a church in Los Angeles for a revival. She tacked up posters on every pole she saw, took out newspaper ads, and did everything she could think of to publicize the event. It was a total bust, but apparently she had kept on asking and looking around, because one day she announced to Clara, "I've found it, I've found it, I've found my church! The Lord put it in my way."

It seems a pastor had died, leaving his congregation on their own; subsequent mismanagement and declining membership had eventually resulted in their putting the building up for sale. Clara said she just sank down into one of the forbidden chairs and cried when she heard the news. This was where she was forced to sing every night—"The Gertrude Ward Miracle Temple for All People." Mom's church. The church that Clara bought. Mom wanted the best, so the best is what Clara had to struggle to pay for: the best Hammond organ, grand piano, pulpit furniture, carpeting, air conditioning, pews, and lighting (luckily, Mom accepted the plumbing and heating as was).

Harry and I had planned a trip to Europe. Our tickets were paid for, and we had enough cash to enjoy our travels without concern—that is, until Mom called four days before the Saturday we were to leave, asking to borrow $500. She sounded so desperate we sent her the money by Western Union. Consequently, our trip was less than it might have been. With that extra cash we could have explored, eaten, and bought more. As it was, we had to watch our expenditures carefully. My daughter Charlotte, who had also moved to California with her children, Buster and Felecia, later told me "Gramm didn't need the money. She just wanted to see if you would send it."

It was Clara who was feeling the pinch. When the church opened, little Felecia would hand out fans, Mom would preach, and Clara would sing her heart and life out. The ingredients were there to ensure a packed house every night, but Christian folk can be most unforgiving; they stayed away in droves, apparently to punish the Wards for working in nightclubs. Some dedicated church members gave as much support as they could, financially and spiritually. They wrote and paid for this declaration to appear in the local newspaper for a month running.

> Sister Gertrude Ward has been instrumental in spiritual guidance in the lives of many and recently organized the Gertrude Ward Miracle Temple for All People, located at 5225 S. Main Street, Los Angeles. Though always busy in propounding the word of Christ, she can boast of playing a major role in the music the world will always love.
>
> For Sister Gertrude Ward, we say that Satan is ever busy and is responsible for the striking of many deadly blows to those dedicated in the work of Christ. Each blow is supposed to make you veer from your path and it is only through such dedicated service as you are giving that you can be strong enough to continue. You must remember Job in the Bible. Even though Satan stripped him of every Earthly possession, including loved ones, God rewarded him for his ever faithful persistence in doing his work. Your reward will be the same.

But the church still did not pay its way, which put continuing pressure on Clara.

WHATEVER the fate of the Miracle Temple, there was no rest for the Miracle Girl. Fifty policemen had to control overflow crowds in Geneva, Switzerland, for the Ward Singers' concerts. From there Clara and her group went on to Germany to do two color specials and to London for six TV appearances, then on to concerts in Rome. Between engagements in Australia, Japan, and South America they taped TV shows in New York and Los Angeles.

I had been keeping busy as well. When my group worked with the Milwaukee Symphony Orchestra in Washington Park, the concert was billed as "Music under the Stars," and the magic was there. Our voices meshed with those of the musical instruments and hung on the warm evening breeze like a tightly woven tapestry. That job was beautiful.

The next day as we headed homeward, Rudy Scott, who was driving for me at the time, turned on the television set in the limousine to Ed Sullivan. The show we had done earlier that year (1969) was being aired, we said almost in unison, "Oh Lord." Memory took us back to the day we had taped it. Clara had asked me to play for the Clara Ward Singers, who were sharing the spotlight with Tony Bennett, Jonathan Winters, and Vicki Carr. Backstage, three of our singers got into an argument. Mom had to separate them to avoid a fist fight. It upset Clara so much she couldn't concentrate on the new material we were doing (the musical director wanted to mix inspirational songs with the Gospel music so that we wouldn't get bogged down in sameness), and we had to retape the song "Born Free" after the audience left. Clara had calmed down by that time and performed perfectly.

FTER three consecutive mishaps on the road, my singers were all but convinced that Mom's prediction was coming true. Clara had overheard Mom talking to herself one night in her bedroom: "That Willa will never have any good luck with that group of hers. They're never gonna make it. You can't do me wrong and get away with it." Clara asked Mom what she thought I was doing or had done to her. It seems she was still stewing over my accepting jobs offered by agents that she and Clara used.

The "hex" was in the joking stage when we missed our appearance at the University of Wisconsin, although the sequence of events on that trip was no joke. Shirley Smith, Rita Bell, Helena Ruffin, Barry Currington (pianist), and I were scheduled to go. The morning of our departure, Helena dropped out. Then Shirley decided there weren't enough singers left to fill out our sound, and she too dropped out. My daughter Charlotte agreed to fill Helena's slot, and after two hours of intense begging, Sandra Peyton said she would go with us.

We did an hour's rehearsing and then took to the road. Barry brought a friend along to drive for us. He was zooming down the Ohio Turnpike at eighty-five miles per hour when we were pulled over by a patrolman. He asked for Barry's friend's driver's license, which we were astounded to find was nonexistent. We cooled our heels at the court-house until daybreak the next morning. We assumed they were trying to nerve us out until we came up with some money. When they were convinced there was none to be had, they let us go.

Sandra and I drove the rest of the way to what we thought was Platteville, Wisconsin, and I called the university to tell them we were in town and would check into our hotel before coming over. "Fine," said the voice on the other end, "we'll be waiting for you." I thought it odd that the operator requested more money than the cost of a local call, but it didn't dawn on us that we were in the wrong town until we'd tried to find the hotel chosen for us. It wasn't there; there was no listing for it in the phone book; and no one we asked knew of such a place. And then the light came on: our destination was still ninety miles away.

Eventually we pulled up at the university, only to be greeted by a sign that read "Willa Ward Concert Canceled." The person in charge told us the decision was made to cancel when we had not arrived by 7:00 P.M. We were so distressed that he told us he would try to resched-ule the concert for the next morning. That made us sleep a bit easier; however, it never happened. I had to pay for our hotel rooms plus $50 to the singers out of my own pocket when we got back to Philadelphia. Sandra drove the first 130 miles homeward before we were stopped again for speeding. After that, I drove all the way back.

A similar problem occurred when we were to open at 9:00 P.M. at the Three Rivers Club in Syracuse, New York. Having gone the wrong way on the turnpike, we arrived just in time for our last show of the night. It was a less than favorable beginning; still the rest of our five-week engagement there was a smashing success.

Then Mr. Boomer booked my group into the Crown and Anchor Inn in Provincetown, Massachusetts, where Clara and Mom had also worked. We opened on Tuesday to a large crowd that swelled to standing-room-only on Wednesday. The patrons were mostly gay and lesbian folks in their twenties and thirties whose wild applause as we entered was an indication of the wonderful reception we were to enjoy for our entire stay. Al, who had tended bar at the Drury Lane in Philadelphia while I was working there, led most of the cheering. I was delighted and surprised to see him there. He invited us to his home for a champagne cocktail party.

With such enthusiastic support we were inspired to sing our best, and our pianist Calvin Statham really pushed those piano keys up and down and around. He and his wife had worked for Mom and Clara before joining me, so when he told me Mom had called him, I assumed it was to wish us well (though it was puzzling that she called him instead of me). That theory collapsed when she began calling him two or three times a day. At first Calvin didn't tell me what was said, but his worried looks showed us something was amiss.

On the Wednesday of our last week at the Crown and Anchor, I opened my motel door to see who was banging on it so hard. A tearful Calvin rushed past me, his arms flailing above his head: "I can't take it, I just can't take it anymore, I'm going crazy." He then broke down and told me how Mom was demanding that he leave me and come out to California because they had a job and just had to have him and no one else. She reminded him that she had put him in "the big time." Through his hysterics and tears, it was evident that he had already succumbed to the barrage of entreaties from the West Coast.

Thursday found Calvin on a plane for California and the rest of us in Provincetown without a pianist. We closed out that evening, leaving Friday and Saturday at the Crown and Anchor empty of our songs, and us just plain empty. We took our disappointment back to Philadelphia.

Calvin had made the mistake of letting Mom know how well we were going over. Clara called later, telling me how Calvin would come to her crying and saying, "I'm so sorry I did Willa that way. She didn't deserve to be treated like that. I'm so sorry."

The "hex" must have lost steam after that, though, because things got better for my group. We were kept busy working festivals and colleges and universities all over the country. Both my daughters sang with my group on these jobs, making them extra nice.

*L*EROY JENKINS and Thea Jones, charismatic healers and evangelists, held a two-week revival at Philadelphia's Metropolitan Opera House on North Broad Street. They always drew thousands of people, and they knew Clara's singing could milk the healing will as well as the goodwill offerings out of the pulsating masses that gathered at the Met. She came and she did! After each meeting there were wet handkerchiefs, crutches, and other aids lying about which the people had tossed into the aisles during the spiritual healing; sometimes the place looked like an infirmary junkyard.

Clara stayed at my house for the two weeks, drinking and sleeping most of her idle time away. She acted and looked drained. I would stand in front of her twice a day making sure she took her medication. She would say, "You're treating me like I'm a baby," or "It's so peaceful here, I dread going back to hearing Mom's mouth." Again, I urged her to stay with me. "I would love to, Will, but I can't. I just can't," said my poor little sister.

I CALLED Clara and Mom to see if they could come to my wedding to Harry Royster on December 10, 1972. Clara said her heart would be with me but she was negotiating with NBC to do a weekly television variety show. It was to be called *The Sheep and the Lambs.* The "sheep" would be secular singers do-

ing voice battles with the Gospel-singing "lambs." She would be the
only constant on the program. There were some details to be worked
out, but she was so sure a contract would be signed in a few days that
she was contemplating buying a $300,000 house across from Nancy
Sinatra's. Clara admitted she was still having bad headaches but wouldn't
go to the doctor because he might tell her not to sing, and that would
blow a golden opportunity.

Two days before my wedding, Clara had a second stroke. Mom said
there was no need for me to come out because she seemed to be coming out of it. A steady flow of faith healers prayed with Clara day and
night. She said they made her more tired than the stroke, but she did.
promise never to drink alcohol again.

My wedding was lovely. Harry and I had designed the ceremony,
but even as it proceeded smoothly, my mind drifted out of my happiness into concern for my sister. Mrs. Bond, whom Mom had sent for to
do the chores and make things easier for everyone, answered the phone
when I called California. I was dumfounded when she told me that
Mom was making Clara play the piano two or three times a day to see
if the stroke had affected her ability. Mom even insisted that she play
fast, difficult numbers as a dexterity test. When Clara complained that
these sessions exhausted her, Mom would respond, "You'll sleep good
tonight." Yet often, when Clara was in a deep sleep, Mom would wake
her up and talk until two or three o'clock in the morning, discussing
what sort of funeral arrangements she wanted should she die.

One day a minister friend called, begging Clara to visit her preacher
father, who had recently suffered an aneurysm. Knowing that Clara had
been healed of a similar condition, she hoped her father would be inspired to be positive and hopeful. My sister definitely wasn't well
enough to make sick calls, but she seized the opportunity to take a brief
respite from Mom. As she put on her boots, to go out, she said, "These
are the ones I wore to Mahalia's funeral. I hope they're not bad luck."
(Our friend Mahalia Jackson had died the year before.)

When she returned from her visit, Clara went right to bed. Later,
wakened by a noise, she found Mom coughing and gasping; a cough-

drop had got stuck in her throat. Clara slapped Mom on the back several times to dislodge the coughdrop, then stepped back saying, "I'm so tired." In an instant, she was a small crumpled mass, lying on the floor in total collapse.

When I arrived in California, I went straight to the hospital. Clara was in a deep coma and had been for a week, her frail body hooked up to a life-support system that kept her hanging on. I went downstairs to call my husband and report on Clara's condition, then got a cup of coffee to take back upstairs with me. I went numb when I saw them wheeling the support equipment out of Clara's room. My little sister had already embarked on a journey through the unknown, leaving behind that tiny, fragile frame in rumpled hospital cap and gown, cold and used up.

I stood there in that hospital room, remembering the last time I had seen my sister prancing to the spirit in sparkling gown and voice. That was at the Harlem Homecoming of the Dance Theatre of Harlem at the Apollo Theater the previous November. Clara had called me and said she and Mom were coming east to be on a big show in New York, and would I be interested in playing the piano for the group. I jumped at the chance. Harry and I, with pianist John Wilson and Rudy Scott, headed up to New York, riding in style in Rudy's limo. In Clara's dressing room at the Apollo, I was shocked to see my sister looking more worn out than ever, but not wanting to rain on her parade, I didn't mention it. We hugged and kissed and dressed for the show, which was indeed star-studded. The list of performers included singer Lena Horne, actress Cicely Tyson, opera star Leontyne Price, jazz singer Carmen McRae, gold record pop group the Fifth Dimension, Oscar-winner Sidney Poitier, singer and TV star Diahann Carroll, movie star Raymond St. Jaques, band leader Cab Calloway, the Clara Ward Singers, and the Peter Duchin Orchestra.

I played the piano along with Peter's band, whose members often looked over at me approvingly. I was really proud. I never heard Clara sing better, although she didn't think so. After the show there was a big party for all the performers at Wilt Chamberlain's club. I wanted to go so much, but the men I had come with had to be back for work the next morning.

I had left my dress in the theater dressing room, but Clara sent it to me. How could I know I'd be wearing it to her funeral two months later?

*W*E SHIPPED Clara's body back to Philadelphia for the first of two funeral services honoring the sparrow who had chirped her way into history.

PHILADELPHIA SERVICE OF TRIUMPH
FOR CLARA WARD 1924–1973

RITUALIST—Rev. Samuel L. Spears–Pastor, Ebenezer Baptist Church
MASTER OF CEREMONIES—Rev. Lester C. Smith–Pastor, Mt. Sinai
    Tabernacle Baptist Church
PROCESSION—"Abide with Me."
SELECTION—Faith Tabernacles–Mutchmore Memorial Baptist
    Church Choir
SCRIPTURE—121 Psalm—Rev. James S. Hall, Jr.–Pastor, Triumph
    Baptist Church
PRAYER—Rev. J. E. Adkins–Pastor, Mt. Ephraim Baptist Church
SELECTION—Nearer My God to Thee—Massed Choirs of
    Philadelphia. Directed by Walter Stewart
REMARKS—Honorable Frank L. Rizzo–Mayor, City of Philadelphia
    represented by Donald K. Angell Jr., Deputy City Representative
    and Director of Commerce Rev. H. J. Trapp–Pastor, Thankful
    Baptist Church
        —Rev. W. E. Cook–President, Baptist Ministers Conference
        —Rev. Leon H. Sullivan–Pastor, Zion Baptist Church
        —Rev. Austin Jefferson–Pastor, Abyssinian Baptist Church

—Rev. W. H. Anderson–Pastor, N.E. Baptist Church

SELECTION—"Soona Will Be Gone"—Clara Ward Singers

REMARKS—Rev. W. L. Bentley–Pastor, Emmanuel Institutional Baptist Church

—Rev. Thea F. Jones–Pastor, Philadelphia Evangelistic Center

—Rev. Leonard Carr–Pastor, Vine Memorial Baptist Church

SOLO—"Too Close"

—Alex Bradford

RESOLUTION—Faith Tabernacle Baptist Church

SELECTION—"Wake Up in Glory"

—Massed Choirs of Philadelphia

SOLO—"Precious Lord"

—Mary Johnson Davis Small

REMARKS—Rev. C. L. Franklin–Pastor, New Bethel Baptist Church, Detroit, Michigan

—Rev. Sandy F. Ray–Pastor, Cornerstone Baptist Church, Brooklyn, New York

OBITUARY—Mrs. Ruth Irvin

SOLO—"Amazing Grace"—Clara Ward Singers (recording)

Eulogy—Rev. E. T. Lewis–Pastor, Mutchmore Memorial Baptist Church

SOLO—"The Day Is Past and Gone"

—Aretha Franklin

RECESSIONAL—"I've Done My Work"

—Clara Ward Singers (recording)

BENEDICTION—Rev. A. W. Swift–Pastor, Gibson Temple Baptist Church

This is in part what was written in a memorial tribute to Clara in the *Gospel Gazette* by one of the mourners:

Quietly, solemnly, they came—from the North, South, East and West making their way to Philadelphia to the Met, the former concert hall recently turned into a church. On this sad day, Sunday, January 22nd, [1973], we paid homage to a child of the King, the late Clara Ward.

Reminiscing, remembering the smile on the face of a woman of slight build, a warm enigmatic personality. Almost hearing that strong beautifully clear voice lifting to the rafters of churches throughout the nation, . . . reaching toward Heaven itself [as] it summoned the Holy Spirit down to bless each soul within hearing. . . .

Our gospel music has reached new dimensions because of Clara. She and others have made the world stop and give due recognition to the music of our heritage. . . . As Brother Walter Stewart approaches the podium to direct the mass choir (composed of choirs and gospel singers of the city), a hush permeates the air as their voices lift in the singing of "Nearer, My God, to Thee," while the family enters.

We are now aware of Clara Ward in the bronze coffin, regally clad in a silver and gold gown. The scripture [prayers,] and remarks were given by many prominent ministers of the area.

Professor Alex Bradford, before singing "Too Close to Heaven," recalled singing this same song for the first time on the anniversary of the Ward Singers. One of the favorites of Clara was the song "Wake Up in Glory." Evangelist Rosie Wallace Brown lifted the mourners almost to glory with her stirring rendition. Brother Walter Stewart directed the mass choir in the up-tempo shout number "We Shall Be Changed." Miss Kitty Parham, a former Ward Singer, sang the lead. . . . The promise of this song seemed to lift the family and 7,000 friends out of the depths of gloom and the spirit made many join in the holy dance. . . . A most unusual thing took place—the voice of Clara Ward singing "Amazing Grace" was heard from a recording. Hearing Clara's voice caused the mood to change. The heaviness now creeps in our hearts and eyes are full with tears. My eyes search the audience for Mother Gertrude Ward. . . . I watch her wringing her hands. She is saying without speaking a word, "Lord, I know your will must be done, but let me hold this moment and my child a little longer." My eyes move over to Willa, Clara's sister, and I see a usually lovely face contorted and glistening with salty tears.

[Philadelphia radio personality] Mary Mason introduces Miss Aretha Franklin. Tonight there is no smile on this young lady's face, for she has lost a friend. [She] sings "The Day Is Past and Gone." At this point, our hearts falter under the weight of sorrow—the full reality is upon us. "The Queen of Gospel Is Gone." Each time a voice is lifted in a song that Clara Ward wrote or inspired, each time a singer enters the realm of music once unthought for gospel, we remember, "Though she is dead, yet she speaks."

It was a sad day in Philadelphia, and I'm told that people cried the world over. We received thousands of cards and telegrams of condolence; I can't begin to list them, but it seemed that everyone from Oral Roberts to Sammy Davis Jr. to former President Lyndon Johnson sent messages. Some two thousand people came to my house after the service and kept coming well into the night.

Mom had always been a kind of expert on funerals. She would go by limo, plane, train, or bus to attend one, taking it as a personal challenge to distract the Devil from claiming the soul of the deceased. She would wear her finest fur, most elaborate hat, and brightest jewels. She would cry, moan, sing, and sway. She would say, "You ain't getting this one, Satan. Try me, do battle with me." If Ruth and Thelma Davis, Dinah Washington, Roberta Martin, Sam Cooke, Mahalia Jackson, and others are in Heaven, perhaps they can in part thank Mom.

At Clara's funeral in Philadelphia, however, I saw my mother weak and vulnerable for the first time, even as she prayed with trembling force.

HE CALIFORNIA "Going Home Service of Praise and Thanksgiving" for Clara was written up this way by Cleveland Banton, reporter for the *Gospel News Journal*:

It had been announced that the remains of Miss Clara Ward would be put on public view at 12 noon on Friday, January 26, 1973, at Harrison and Ross Mortuary. By 10 A.M. a mass of people had already gathered outside the Mortuary to pay their last respects to the Queen of Gospel Music.

It was here on the outskirts of Los Angeles that Clara Ward had made her home during the past five years. She had made many friends here. . . .

She touched the lives of many, many thousands that heard her sing.

So now they came with tear-stained eyes and heavy hearts. They came remembering the joy and hope that her music had brought to the world the past 43 years. A steady line of mourners filed past her open coffin until 6 P.M., when Miss Ward's body was taken to beautiful Shrine Auditorium for her final "Going Home Service."

A contingent of ministers representing various religious orders were there to give praise and thanksgiving for the life of their fallen queen. . . .

Several recordings of Clara's voice were played ("Amazing Grace" and "Beams of Heaven"). The thousands of mourners sat, stood, ran, and shouted. "Yes, Lord." "Thank You Jesus." "Hallelujah." The pinnacle of emotion was reached as the recording "Surely, God Is Able" was played, for this. . . . had earned the Ward Singers their first gold disc. . . . Marion Williams, who was part of the Ward Singers during the making of this disc and also shared the lead, reached out to Mrs. G. Ward and continued to shout "Surely, Surely, Surely, God Is Able to Carry You Through."

Under the direction of Rev. James Cleveland, a mass choir consisting of over one hundred voices sang several soul stirring songs made famous by the Ward Singers, [including] "Precious Memories" and "Packin' Up Lord, Gettin' Ready To Go."

An array of present and former Ward Singers formed their own choir composed of eighteen or more members. They joined in singing "We Shall Be Changed" and "The Day Is Past and Gone."

Mom Ward, overcome with emotions, stood and reminisced [about] Clara's last earthly days. "On Watch Meeting Night (December 31, 1972)," Mother Ward recalled, "I asked Clara to sing me a song, . . . 'My Soul Looks Back and Wonders How I Got Over.' Clara said 'Mother that's not the song I would like to sing for you.' She then sat down at the piano and sang 'When the Storms of Life Are Raging,

Stand by Me.' That was the last song Clara ever sang. She passed on
to a better land on January 16, 1973."

The following morning a cortege of cars lined four city blocks to go
that last mile with Clara as she was taken to the Forest Lawn Memorial
Park and laid to rest in a crypt in the Forest Memorial Mausoleum,
where Gracie Allen, Nat "King" Cole, and other "greats" have also been
laid to rest. ABC-TV taped portions of the funeral services.

My granddaughter Felecia was a blessing through it all, showing so
much maturity and strength. I know there would have been turmoil getting things done without her tireless efforts.

Unfortunately, the question of money was a jarring note at Clara's
death, as it had been during her life. Mom told us she didn't have
enough for the funeral repast, so—as in Philadelphia—that expense fell
on Harry and me in California, though Marion Williams helped too. Of
Clara's $30,000 insurance policy, Mom spent $20,000 on funeral
arrangements and flowers. The remaining $10,000, she said, was used
for "incidentals." My cousin Mary told me that Clara had left me some
money but that Mom said she wasn't going to give it to me. I didn't ask
her about it. Whenever she needed money, I sent it to her until she died.

HEN WE had all settled down after high sorrow,
it was back to business as usual. I asked Mom if I
could take over as head of Clara's group, with her
as manager. I wanted to keep the name "the Clara Ward Singers" alive.
Mom said she would think about it. In anticipation, I set up a recording date and contacted several agents. When I told Mom the steps I had
taken, she was furious. "You trying to take over already. It'll never happen." That was the end of that.

Because of her reaction to my proposal, I was surprised when Mom called me to come to California to rehearse for an album of Clara's original songs with her singers: Viola Crowley, Agnes Jackson, Vermida Royster, Madeline Thompson, Alice Houston, and Adele Schofield, with Freddy Daniels on piano. I swallowed my pride and flew out to L.A.

The folks from the Merrill Lynch investment firm were backing the project; they had offered Mom $35,000 for the use of the Clara Ward name and singers in commercials and promotions, plus $10,000 per concert or taping. A Mr. Barr, who was the agent handling everything, gave us two weeks to achieve the same sound as the group had when Clara was singing. Of course that was impossible—nobody could take Clara's place—but we came fairly close after rehearsing day and night. We each had solo songs that fit our voices. My big one was "I Heard the Voice of Jesus Say." When Mr. Barr came to hear and judge the results of our efforts, we were as ready as we could get. He thought we sounded wonderful. He was making notes as we went through our paces, and when we were through, he started talking arrangements and money.

Mom wanted to talk to him in private so we couldn't hear what was being said, but he wanted to address the whole group. He began by saying there would always be a full orchestra complete with strings to accompany us. When he mentioned money, Mom tried again to isolate him, to no avail. Agnes spoke up: "Stop trying to tell Mr. Barr how to run things. If he wants us to hear what he has to say, why not?" Mom blew up and started cursing everybody out. Agnes said, "You're senile," and then Mom really went off.

Mr. Barr stared in disbelief. "Well that's it. You're so smart—now nobody'll use the Clara Ward name. The deal's off." I told him he could use my group, but by then he didn't want to get involved any further. He took his proposal and left. For good.

Mom had had a dual purpose for having me come to Los Angeles. She had planned a memorial for Clara at her church. I didn't like the idea because I thought she was doing it mostly to get new members.

The turnout was small, partly because a freak storm suddenly blew in with heavy sleet and snow. I was glad Clara couldn't see how few came to memorialize a woman who had pulled Gospel singing from local black churches and spread it lovingly over the universe—Clara Ward, "the Miracle Girl."

Mom spoke and we sang; then Mom put on a record of Clara singing "I've Done My Work." The surprise of hearing her voice on top of missing her so much was more than my composure could take. I snatched the record off the turntable and yelled, "She sang herself to death and no one cares; let her rest in peace in death. She surely couldn't rest in life." Mom cried crocodile tears, but for the first time, she didn't scream at me. The next day she called various people who had been there to make excuses for me, telling them I was overcome with grief.

*T*HE TRUTH was that I just couldn't stand to have my sister used *again*. After all those exhausting years of unending work, all that was left of Clara's estate were her lovely house in Baldwin Hills and the church she bought for my mother (both of which my mother soon lost), a fur coat, a diamond ring, a few dresses and suits, and a small bank account.

I also found a notebook with brief impressions and observations— some a bit cryptic—of people she had known over the years:

THE DIXIE HUMMINGBIRDS
Loads of fun, told good jokes. Glad they moved to Philadelphia.
PROF. DORSEY
Looks good for his age, can really sing blues.
SALLIE MARTIN
Mean and Sassy.

REVEREND MARTIN L. KING AND REV. GRAY, 2ND, are really good
   friends. They make you confident when they discuss where we've
   been and where we're going. Could listen to them endlessly.
MAHALIA JACKSON
   I wish I could roll my skinny belly the way she does. Beautiful
   person.
LITTLE SIS (ROSETTA THARPE)
   A nut. Fun! Fun! Fun!
ALEX BRADFORD AND ALBERTA
   Moves me singing. Is he or isn't he?
MY BABY ARETHA
   She doesn't know how good she is. Doubts self. Some day ——
   — to the moon. I love that girl.
JOAN CRAWFORD
   Hard-looking, but beautiful.
JOE LOUIS
   Nice man, but dumb. The government did him dirty. They
   took all his money even though he gave so much to war effort.
   Now they're taking care of the countries we defeated.
SIS CUNNINGHAM
   Ugly – – – –
JAMES CLEVELAND
   Like to see him do his gimmicks and holy dance. Thinks he's
   cute.
RUTH (DINAH WASHINGTON)
   When she sings um—um —. It makes you think of all the erotic
   things you ever thought involving your special person. I
   wonder why she always sucks ice?
ELLA FITZGERALD
   I, softy, cried when the band didn't back her the way she
   wanted.
NAT KING COLE
   Stands backstage, away from everyone, really shy.
EDNA G. COOK
   I think she and Mom liked the same preacher.
EARTHA KITT
   Surprising, warm and sociable.

It was a long list.

Of course, Clara's real legacy is her music, which will live on in tribute to my sister, the greatest (to my mind) writer of Gospel songs in the twentieth century.

Without Clara's money, though, it was impossible for Mom to keep the bills up. The house and church were both lost, and she moved into an apartment that was a far cry from the home she had become accustomed to. When times change, they often take past gains along. One dreadful night, an apartment fire licked up what was left of Mom's opulent past.

$\mathcal{M}$Y MOTHER put together a male Ward Singers group and brought them east to do a concert at Mutchmore Memorial Baptist Church. Whenever Mom came to Philly, she always stayed with Harry and me, and this time Acey came to my house to see her. Harry and I were on our way to attend a formal affair given by Los Hernandos Social Club.

We returned home from a grand evening to find Mom shaking and sobbing. There were bruises on her neck. After a bit of prodding, she told us that Acey had tried to rape her—we doubted that he only "tried." Even though Harry swore he would never allow Acey in the door again, Mom would never stay at my house after that. Long after Mom had left, Acey would call saying he was going to kidnap Mom and me and make us his sex slaves. He kept that up for three years. A year later Acey was dead, but Mom carried to her grave the terror he had instilled in her.

The Male Ward Singers never drew large crowds. Gertrude Ward had come full circle: they were singing for freewill offerings. Mom had started to live in the past, thinking of herself still as a mover and shaker. After the fire she came back to Philly and moved in with Rudy Scott, our former chauffeur, who was living in the southwest part of town. He was such a kindly, easygoing man that Mom could easily handle him. Before long, Rudy's home was not his own. Mom insisted he get rid of his furniture to make room for the pieces she had in storage. Poor Rudy was not allowed to look at his own television set or listen to popular music on his radio—that is, until he had finally had enough and began putting on both TV and radio at the same time.

Mom left in a huff, taking all the furniture with her. But when the movers started to take the kitchen set, Rudy said, "Over my dead body. You made me get rid of all my furniture—you're going to leave me something to eat on," and he picked up a kitchen knife to emphasize his determination. They all got the point and got the hell out of there, Mom calling over her shoulder as she left, "I'll get you for this. You won't have any peace." Rudy was so angry with Mom, he put out with the trash loads of one-of-a-kind records and photographs that can never be replaced.

Mom disbanded her men's group and went back to California, where she got another apartment and tried to start up the female Ward Singers again. But the peak had passed. Agents and managers were fed up with her constant interference and argumentative nature. They had taken her abuse when the group meant big bucks for them, but without Clara it was intolerable.

*M*Y CLUB work had been going smoothly until 1978, when black entertainers were for a time systematically locked out of work in downtown and suburban Philadelphia nightclubs. Even those who had worked the circuit for years were caught up in the us-against-them mess, and white patrons stopped going to clubs that hired blacks. Financial difficulties at home even drove me to seek domestic work, but without references, that outlet was closed to me as well.

Booking agent Lee Rendi, my friend of twenty years, kept trying until she found a club willing to give me a chance: Charles Judson, owner of Christopher's in Ambler, Pennsylvania, agreed to let me audition. An audition—after years of working such class houses in the area as the Latin Casino, Arthur's Steak House, and the Marriott Hotel! Still, despite misgivings about whether his patrons would accept me, Judson gave me a six-night trial. It was a degrading situation, but I jumped at the chance. Joe Gregory, Rita Bell, Toni Rose, and I really socked it to them, and for the next three and a half years we played to standing-room-only crowds. We were back!

During that time, I was offered a lucrative job as a single at Caesar's Boardwalk Regency Casino in Atlantic City, but I was having so much fun and we were so well liked at Christopher's that I decided to stay put with my group.

I was working in New York City when my daughter Charlotte called to tell me that Mom had taken sick. I terminated my job, stopped at home to grab some fresh clothes, and flew out to Los Angeles. Mom was weak but lucid. She was at her own apartment but still needed plenty of bed rest and care. I asked her to move back to Philadelphia with me, but that idea seemed to upset her, so I let it alone. After calling around and finding that nursing homes were prohibitively expensive, I asked Marion Williams if she would come out to take care of Mom for a while, and she answered yes. Marion did all she could, but the arrangement soon became too much for her. Mom had become very demanding and more cantankerous than ever.

After Marion left, Mark Tyson—a Gospel soloist from New Jersey—stepped in to become essentially a servant to my mother, who was losing weight and strength. Madeline Thompson too waited on her till the end. At last she had to be rushed to the hospital, severely dehydrated. When I walked into her hospital room my heart sank. She could neither talk nor walk; she had tubes everywhere, and a catheter bag was full of blood. It didn't look hopeful, so I had stayed at the hospital all night. At 6:30 A.M. on November 27, 1981, in all forgiveness and love, I saw my mother, Gertrude Murphy Ward, slip silently on bared feet past the mortal station and, I like to hope, into the Heaven she had sung about all her born days.

I found a large cardboard box whose contents shed some light on where a lot of Mom's money had gone. There were ninety-seven money order stubs, some of them yellow with age. Their amounts ranged from $50 to $500, all made out to radio and television ministries. Mom had probably used money orders rather than personal checks to hide the transactions from Clara. The box also held small icons, crosses, and prayer cloths. Prayer cloths are small squares of red fabric which are "blessed" and sent to financial donors with the promise that they will aid in bettering poor health and habits and (ironically) erasing financial worries.

When I opened Mom's safe deposit box I was shocked to find only a life insurance policy in the grand sum of $2,000. My husband and I added to that amount to give Mom a fitting funeral. Charlotte helped me with the casket selection. People still think that my sister and mother left a fortune behind. If they did, it's gathering dust or interest somewhere, or someone is living well because of it. There are folks who believe Mom squirreled money away or entrusted it to an unscrupulous lawyer or friend.

The funeral services were held on December 2, 1981, at Victory Baptist Church in Los Angeles. Mom accomplished in death what had escaped her at the end of her singing and preaching career: the church was full to overflowing. She was buried in the same mausoleum as Clara, at Forest Lawn Cemetery. Her obituary, as it appeared in the program for her Going Home Service, reads in part:

> Through the divinely inspired leadership of Mother Ward (as she became affectionately known) and under her strict management, the World-Famous Ward Singers became the number-one gospel group in the world. One who in less than an hour's notice, could fill up concert halls and arenas without benefit of advance publicity, Madam Ward was also the first Black female booking agent in the world and guided her singers into stardom through their classic recording of the first "Million Seller" gospel record "Surely God Is Able."

Further, she was singlehandedly responsible for the introduction and recognition of numerous theretofore unheard of singers, many of whom have enjoyed lucrative careers through Madam Ward's exposure.

In 1957, Madam Ward conceived and organized the nation's first gospel cavalcade, featuring the Famous Ward Singers and the six top gospel groups of the day in a cross-country tour stopping in over forty cities.

During the decade of the sixties Madam Ward saw her band of gospel singers rise to even greater popularity, performing for three presidents of the United States, then appearances on all the major television and radio shows . . . and performances in over twenty countries throughout the world. In addition, the Famous Ward Singers enthralled audiences on the leading colleges campuses and in Las Vegas for five years and delighted Disneyland customers . . . with their gospel-style performances. . . .

Mother Ward dearly loved the family and knew beyond a shadow of a doubt that she was deeply loved by them. She considered herself to be an extremely fortunate person, speaking continually of her blessings, telling all who called her on the telephone "Surely God Is Able, hello."

On Friday, November 27, 1981, at 6:35 A.M., in French Hospital, Los Angeles, California, the trumpets of Heaven resounded in a vibrant cantata—the clouds of the sky rolled back; the voices of the angels called the mighty roll and Madam Gertrude Ward ceased her endeavors and closed her eyes to rest until the second coming of the Lord. I've done my work, I've sung my song, I've done some good, I've done some wrong. Now I must go where I belong, the good Lord hath willed it so!

Sleep on, Mother Ward, you've buckled up your traveling shoes, you have packed up, and you're ready to go; your storm has passed over and now you'll greet all of those who enter into the pearly gates, telling them "Surely God Is Able."

Liberace with Clara after she won the West Coast Theatrical Writers'
Best-Dressed Poll, 1967. *Photo by Edward J. Allen Associates, Inc. All photos from the
author's collection.*

George Raft with Clara, backstage in Las Vegas, 1963.

Clara and Duke Ellington at the Hollywood Bowl, 1965.
Photo by Earl Fowler.

Clara and Tom Jones, Las Vegas, 1960s.

Clara (right) with singer Nancy Wilson and Vince Edwards (TV's *Ben Casey*) at a Hollywood party honoring Clara, mid-1960s.

Clara, singer Billy Daniels, and Gertrude, n.d.

Clara saying goodbye to Gladys Bonds and Gertrude, who were leaving from Paris for the Holy Land, 1965.

Gertrude in the Holy Land, December 1965.

The Clara Ward
Singers in
Vietnam, 1966.
Left to right:
bottom, Madeline
Thompson, Clara,
Mildred Means;
top, Mavelyn
Statham, Alton
Williams, Viola
Crowley.

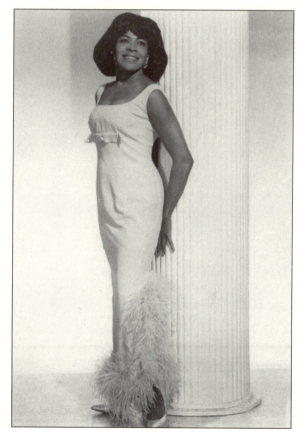

Willa Ward, 1967.
*Photo by Michael
Denning.*

The Willa Ward Singers, 1967. Willa's daughter Rita Bell (left), Willa (seated), Evelyn Vinson (top), Willa's daughter Charlotte Sims (right).

Clara, the "Miracle Girl,"
arriving in Philadelphia
with Gertrude after her
stroke in Miami, 1967.
Photo by Jack T. Franklin.

Willa with Ella Fitzgerald
at a concert for American
Federation of Musicians
Local 802, New York, 1969.
Photo by Archer Associates.

Elvis Presley with the Clara Ward Singers, Las Vegas, 1969. Left to right: Mavelyn Statham, Geraldine Jones, Clara Ward, Elvis Presley, Viola Crowley, Mildred Means, Vermida Royster, Alton Williams (pianist).

Sophie Tucker (center) with Clara and Gertrude in Australia, 1971.

Maurice Chevalier and Clara at the Olympia Theatre, Paris, 1971. Condensed photo from a wide-angle shot.

Willa and Louis
Armstrong backstage at
the Local 802 concert,
1969. *Photo by Archer
Associates.*

Gertrude Ward and
Celestine Jennings
accepting for Clara, at
her posthumous
induction into the
Songwriters' Hall of
Fame, New York, 1974.

Gertrude Ward singing at Ebenezer Baptist Church, Philadelphia, after receiving an award, 1974. *Photo by Ruben E. Hall.*

Willa Ward and her husband Harry J. Royster on the cruise ship *Maxim Gorki*, 1978. *Photo by the ship's photographer.*

Toni Rose and Willa Ward working at Christopher's in Ambler, Pa., 1982.

Epilogue

*S*O NOW there was just Willa Ward.

I approached A. G. Brooks with the idea of staging a Golden Anniversary concert in 1984—fifty years after Mom's first—in celebration and honor of the Famous Ward Singers and in loving tribute to Gertrude and Clara Ward. I was joined by early group members Frances Steadman, Esther Ford, Marion Williams, and (replacing Kitty Parham, who was in the hospital at the time), Rita Palmer. Bright Hope Baptist Church was filled to capacity. The Reverend Louise Williams, as emcee, introduced my other guests: the Philadelphia Male Chorus, the Reverend James C. Edwards, Dorothy Love Coates and the Gospel Harmonettes. Pianist Alberta Bradford played brilliantly—as usual.

The Clara Ward Singers, now based in Los Angeles and managed by Madeline Thompson, are still traveling and performing. In 1992 I gave them permission to record a CD in tribute to Gertrude and Clara Ward and to the Reverend James Cleveland (who trained with Thomas A. Dorsey and was a major Gospel singer and composer until his death in 1991). Their latest release is a CD titled *Meetin' Tonight,* produced in 1994 by the Welk Music Group from tracks recorded for Vanguard LPs. In 1995 I sang with the group at a tribute to Clara organized by James Scott in New Bern, North Carolina. That same year we accepted the James Cleveland Award presented to the Clara Ward Singers on the Gospel Music Stellar Awards television show.

Meanwhile, I went on with club work, and 1987 found me singing at the SAS Scandinavian Hotel in Bergen, Norway. Jean Harris and her husband, entertainers from Canada, heard me there and asked their agent to contact me about working the European circuit with them.

Once back in the States I sent the agent a tape, and in short order I was sitting at the piano in Oslo's plush KNA Park Avenue Hotel. My three-month contract (with options) stipulated alternating appearances in hotels and on a cruise ship sailing from Norway to Germany and back.

The atmosphere was so lovely that I wanted to share it with my husband and, after three weeks, asked Harry to come over and travel with me. His answer: "I've been there once—that's enough. I've seen all I want to see. You come on home." Why I have so often allowed my husbands to disrupt good bookings is beyond me—but I did. My agent was in total shock when I told him I had to go back to America because of a death in my family. He had to cancel the rest of my dates and a scheduled recording session. Once again my forward motion was impeded: that agent would not book me again, and so another marvelous connection was severed.

When I came home, people said, "Willa, you left that good job because you don't need the money." Contrary to popular belief, however, I live quite modestly. I receive writer's royalties from ten original songs, but the royalties from the bulk of Clara's music go to Herman Lubinsky of Planemar Music Company, who bought the publishing rights years ago. Mom was told that production and advertising costs had to be met before any revenue would be forthcoming, and then it would be minimal. My mother was grossly misled. The company is still raking it in from Clara's music.

Toni Rose and I were packing them in at the Trolley stop in Shippack, Pennsylvania, when my doctor told me I should have a nodule removed from my vocal cords. Then, after we'd explained to the club owner why we had to quit the job (and he'd actually gone down on his knees to beg us to stay), the doctor changed his mind; he didn't want to do the procedure after all, because it might end my career as a singer.

And so I kept singing. In 1989 I sang in New York's Central Park at a huge Gospel happening for which Marion Williams was contracted. Kitty Parham and Frances Steadman rounded out our group. Marion was most gracious in announcing to the vast audience that my family had been responsible for giving her her first chance and worldwide exposure. Later, we joined Marion for a songfest in Atlanta, Georgia.

In 1995, an eventful year for me, Frances, Kitty, Esther Ford, and I—in the name of the Famous Ward Singers—were featured guests at an anniversary celebrated by Johnny Thompson, international Gospel arranger and promoter. We also sang at the National Convention of Gospel Choirs and Choruses (founded by Thomas A. Dorsey). And I was invited to the opening of the Rock-and-Roll Hall of Fame in Cleveland, Ohio, accompanied by Toni Rose (musician, artist, and the writer who has helped me put this book together) and Vera Gunn (a public relations person). What would Mom think if she could see the Ward Singers' books, stage clothes, and other artifacts that are on display in the museum there?

It was especially satisfying in October of that year to take part in the ten-day grand opening festivities at the brand-new home of the Philadelphia Clef Club of Jazz and the Performing Arts. It was my pleasure to perform at the Sunday afternoon jazz concert with the Evelyn Simms Quartet. Evie has been in demand as a singer from the age of fifteen, performing and touring with many of the legendary names in show business. Though we didn't know each other at the time, she and I as young girls had frequented many of the same places, and we had worked together in Atlantic City years before. On this grand occasion, in the company of multitudes of today's "name" musicians, we showed that the ol' girls are still kicking it. Yahoo!

The Clef Club's new quarters, according to its newsletter *Treble Clef,* are

> the culmination of a dream that many of its members carried over the years from the time the original Clef Club functioned as the social conduit of the Black wing of Local 274 of the then segregated American Federation of Musicians. The prime keeper of this dream was noted drummer and promoter Bill "Mr. C" Carney. . . . In 1984 "Mr. C" shared his vision of a facility devoted to the presentation and instruction of jazz with Dr. Bernard Watson, then president and CEO of the William Penn Foundation. Fortunately . . . Watson was an old jazz player who appreciated Philadelphia's role in jazz history.

Our Local 274, chartered in 1935, had its union hall at 912 South Broad, which was for years *the* place to hear great sounds and rub shoul-

ders with many of the finest musicmasters going. When the Civil Rights
Act of 1964 outlawed segregated unions, we knew that our control and
uniqueness would evaporate in a merger with the formerly all-white Local 77. Local 274's last president, Jimmy Adams, and other former members tried to preserve some of the union's advantages by keeping up the
Clef Club as a social organization. But there were operational difficulties and a constant struggle to maintain adequate quarters—until "Mr.
C" persuaded Watson to come on board.

Finally (dreams do come true!), thanks to the mighty efforts of many
individuals—and the support of the William Penn Foundation and
other charitable, cultural, and business organizations—a four-story,
multimillion-dollar building dedicated to the preservation and promotion of jazz is now part of the city's Avenue of the Arts. It houses a two-
story performance hall, classrooms and practice rooms, a library and
archive. I wish Mom and Clara could see it.

I live alone now. My husband Harry Royster passed away after a lin-
gering illness. On Tuesday, January 5, 1993, he entered into his eternal
rest. Recently I was diagnosed as having a heart condition, but at this
point it does not seem life-threatening as long as I continue my medication. I finally had that nodule removed from my vocal cord, which
diminished my singing capacity a bit, but I still play on Gospel programs, at nursing homes, and each week at the Senior Center in the
Park, in Philadelphia's Germantown.

Both my daughters are productive, active young women with good
jobs. For a brief time, Rita led her own interracial band and did gigs as
a pianist and singer on the East Coast. Charlotte lives in Los Angeles
with her young son, Larry Jr. Felecia, her daughter, is a new bride, married to Navy man Terrance Bell.

I want to close with messages to members of this family of mine,
major players in the drama of the Ward Singers and in my life.

To my sister and friend, Clara

From as early as I can remember, the all of you was delicate and frail—
even your initiative was far from robust.

When you started to sing as a little girl, I was too close and too young to know how very special your talent was. But you inherently knew.

When cruel jokes were made by your schoolmates about your "skinny legs and funny face," you swore through tears and resolution that one day they would look up to you and proudly brag to folks what a great friend you were.

Many of those with experience recognized your potential and ready talent as they sought you out for appearances (much to the chagrin of some seasoned singers and pianists who were passed by). In time, your face, spirit, and voice were known and easily recognized the world over. As a European columnist wrote,

> Clara Ward, that tiny-framed gospel singer from across the sea, has the strength of delivery and purpose to open portals that were "bolted" by prejudice, tumble walls that separated dissimilar brethren from brethren, melt hearts that had been galvanized by pain or anguish.

My little Clara, my fragile little Clara, you boldly took on the world and won it with your glorious presentations of Gospel on musical wings.

Between restful intervals, let your spirit soar and, now and then, sing "How I Got Over"—just for me.

I miss you dearly.

Always,
Willa

To my father, George Ward

In all our time—despite all the chaos—you were the stabilizing force. Daddy, you held our lives together in such an unobtrusive manner, we hardly noticed that our existence might very well have come unglued without you.

We didn't realize, at the time, how important your being there for us was.

I hope there were instances where one or all of us drove the reality of your great worth to your consciousness.

Love,
Willa

To my mother, Gertrude A. M. Ward

I was told as a child that you had suffered a nervous breakdown. It was offered at a time when you were "acting out." The explanation, I'm sure, was to rationalize your frequent spells of bizarre behavior. Through the years, I have pumped relatives about the intensity and devastation of the illness but never got any concrete information. There were times when the illness theory was easier to accept than just plain meanness.

What prompted the wild mood swings will never be resolved; however, the solid facts of your remarkable accomplishments are undisputable.

Whatever the force was that drove you, it took you to regions and heights that many singers are still capitalizing on today.

You took everything past the limits that society had set. You drew your own lines, created your own perimeters—which, from time to time, you yourself bounded over.

The nature of genius is vastly misunderstood by the masses. The jump-started kick-in place for those so endowed is well beyond where most of us have already done our all and quit.

Your cutting edge sliced open a path of acceptance of Gospel music that is ever widening, ever building on the foundation you laid down.

No, Ma, you are not to be explained. In the final analysis, you are to be praised.

Love,
Willa

To my daughters, Charlotte Moultrie Sims and Rita Moultrie Bell

I don't think you have a clue what joy you gave to your dad and me. You were good girls and I'm grateful for that—even though I remember spanking you at regular intervals to keep the "Devil out of you." This was the way I was raised; however, I thank God I came to my senses and realized how wrong and hurtful the practice was.

When I was working on the road, I missed you girls tremendously. I tried to make up for my absence by taking you to fun places and providing you with as many pleasant diversions as I knew of and could afford. My love for you was always there.

Through it all, you both turned out beautifully. I'm truly proud.

Love ya!

Mom

Afterword, Appendix, and Index

Gospel Music Hall of Fame

TO all to whom these presents may come Greetings be it known now and for time immemorial that the conferring of this honor is the highest tribute to mortal accomplishment in the field of gospel music and yet, it is but a grain in the sands of time and the presence of God.

The members and friends of the gospel music industry and the Board of Directors and membership of the Gospel Music Association do hereby pay tribute to the accomplishments and spirit of selfless dedication that have touched the lives of millions through the spreading of the True Word and the Good News.

Whereas, there has been established by the Gospel Music Association an institution devoted to recognizing and honoring those few bright lights who have illuminated the paths of millions through their music; and

Whereas, by action of the President and Chairman of the Board of Directors of the Gospel Music Association and by action of the Hall of Fame Committee the Hall of Fame electors, the general membership of the Gospel Music Association and friends of gospel music everywhere; and

Whereas, this great light of gospel music has been judged by peers on earth to be worthy of memorial recognition by reason of indelible impact on the annals of gospel history; and

Whereas, this great light has evidenced the qualities of accomplishment necessary to obtain the approbation of the Grand Architect of the Universe with regard to gospel activity, influence in time or significance and selfless devotion, both in professional and personal life;

Know Ye that we, pursuant to an act of our assembled bodies do hereby invite, admit and induct

Clara Ward

into the membership of the Gospel Music Hall of Fame to share in all rights and privileges appertaining thereto; and

In testimony whereof, we have caused these names to be made patent and our great seal to be hereunto affixed the 3rd day of April in the 209th year of our independence and in the year of our Lord, Nineteen Hundred eighty-five.

Afterword

Excerpts from an Interview with John Wilson

*T*HE WARD SINGERS' side members (Esther, Marion, Kitty, Frances, and Mrs. Waddy) left the group after a long period of money disputes. They didn't think they were getting their fair share of the take. The idea was to start their own group. A couple of them felt they were the stars and that they would get to the top like the Wards or better. Well, they started out real good when they went to Europe to do the play *Black Nativity*. After that, they didn't do anything of note.

On the other hand, when the Wards got the new group hooked up, there was no stopping them. The first big program was at the Philadelphia Metropolitan Opera House. They had to turn folks away. And so it went.

Aretha Franklin came to Philly to sing at the Showboat Club on Lombard Street. After checking in at the hotel upstairs over the club, she took a cab over to Mom Ward's house to get connected to familiar souls. She was a little nervous about breaking into pop singing. That night Clara, me, and Rudy (the Wards' chauffeur) went to the Showboat to catch Aretha's performance.

The only people familiar with the name Aretha Franklin were Gospel people, who weren't about to show up. They were angry at her crossing over to pop. When we went in the door we heard that wonderful voice and saw that it was being wasted on an almost empty house.

Note: I am grateful to John Wilson, one of our pianists and a long-time friend who worked with the various Ward groups from time to time, for sharing and allowing me to record his memories and perspectives. John started out as a kind of "groupie" who idolized Clara and worked very hard to develop his talent and Gospel repertoire. John's last words to me after our taping session in 1986 were, "Make sure I'm in that book!" He died of AIDS five months later.

Aretha's face lit up with gratefulness when she saw Clara. On her intermission, Aretha's eyes welled up with tears as she said, "These people
don't want to hear me, I still sound like I'm in church." "Well, Aretha,"
answered Clara, "if you can't sing before these few, you'll never sing before thousands. You keep playing and singing like you're doing and one
day this place won't be able to hold the people. Look at us, how we
started." "Yes, Clara that's easy for you to say. You're on your way to
Vietnam and you were just on the Ed Sullivan show. I ain't been
nowhere."

Clara said, "You just hang in there—you've got everything it takes
to go to the top. You'll have them hanging on to every word, every
note."

When Clara and Mom were at Disneyland, Rudy and I drove out to
California to see them. We registered at the Clark Hotel. Two days
later, Mom Ward said, "Get on out of that sleazy hotel and come stay
at the house. How would you like to play for us while you're here?" I
was in shock. Vi[ola Crowley] had gotten involved with some guy and
wasn't showing up on time for the job. After coming down from the
clouds, I said, "Mom, I would like to play for you at Disneyland, but I'm
not in the union. " Mom Ward answered, "Don't worry about it. I'll take
care of that."

Mom had the girls all thinking she was a monster, but I saw she had
a soft spot in her heart by living with her. Clara did more of the business than many people realized. I'd hear her on the phone deciding
what to do about this or that. She would say, "Mom, you have to take
care of this or that." Sometimes Mom would like a singer but Clara
would say, "No, that voice won't fit with our sound." Since she had to
mold and train the girls, she knew exactly what was what.

Some of the girls said Mom wouldn't pay them, but I always got
paid. Except for Yankee Stadium. Most, in fact, all of the singers I knew
at that time came from poor backgrounds. Sometimes when they said
they didn't get paid, they meant they didn't get what they thought the
most famous Gospel groups of all time would pay. They had dreams of
getting out of the ghetto and into houses with pools and such. It didn't

work like they wanted it to, but they got a chance to go see places they wouldn't have seen in a lifetime or meet people of high station. It's nobody's fault that they didn't reach the heights they thought they could. If they had anything going outside of the Ward Singers, they would have taken it and gone. Just like Marion Williams. Mrs. Ward put her on top of the world. She was good, but she would not have had the exposure without the Wards—she would have still been singing in neighborhood churches. How soon we forget. I've heard her put down Mrs. Ward. Well, that's how it goes. I know in Disneyland the girls were making $325 a week. That was in 1966 when I was there. Mrs. Ward took the group as far as she could, but manager Monte Kay, who also managed Flip Wilson, took them all the way. He had dealings with millionaires and heads of governments. The only other Gospel star that was doing anything was Mahalia, but even she couldn't go where the Ward Singers could go.

When people talk about Mahalia not working clubs, that's true, but when she got big she would not work small churches either; she was above that. But Mother Ward and Clara could and would work concert halls tonight and a storefront the next night. Mom felt because you were poor, you still were entitled to hear them sing. "You don't have to have money to sing about and praise the Lord," she said. At the clubs we worked, no whiskey was served while we were performing. Mom wouldn't have it. They brought in so much business, the management went for it.

Everybody came to see Clara at the New Frontier (in Vegas). James Cleveland brought out a group with him. He said, "Lord, would I love to work out there." But the Wards had that so nobody could touch them. The folks would be lined up around the pavilion. It was impossible to get a seat if you didn't get there for the first wave.

Mrs. Ward would sit on stage with what I call her skunk wig (it had a wide white stripe up the front). She would be giving instructions all during the show. "Hold that note." "Get those feet up." "Tighten up."

When Clara came back from Vietnam, I don't know if it was the first or second trip, but she was scheduled to do the Isley Brothers show at

Yankee Stadium called "It's Your Thing." She also did a crusade program with the Reverend Leroy Jenkins.

Mrs. Ward had an all-male group called the Los Angeles All Stars. Charles May was in the group and they did backup for Quincy Jones. When I was in California in 1966, Clara was really having trouble with her blood pressure. Some nights her head hurt so bad she couldn't go to work. There was a woman who used to take her pressure. "Clara, you got to do something, it's too high." Clara would say, "I'll go to sleep, it'll be all right." Even when Clara was hurting, she still tried to joke. Mom would ask Clara, "You been drinking again?" Mom Ward always dominated Clara, but when it came to business, Clara would put her foot down many times. Mrs. Ward knew when to back off, because Clara had good instincts and Mom knew it.

Back on the East Coast we did a lot of colleges. Willa's group took some of the jobs. While we were on that end, we did the Jerry Blavitt TV show. Willa, Al [Williams], and Skeets Marsh worked with us on that one. I remember when we did the Mike Douglas TV show, I was so thrilled to meet Shirley Bassey, who was also a guest artist. Clara asked me if I wanted to meet her. I said, "Yes! Yes!" I know that they took movies of Clara in Vietnam. I wonder what happened to that film?

The Harlem Homecoming was a fabulous affair. That one was on television too. There was Cab Calloway, Leontyne Price, Lena Horne, Diahann Carroll, Carmen McCrae, Sidney Poitier, Peter Duchin and his orchestra, the Clara Ward Singers. After it was over, we went to Wilt Chamberlain's club. Real groovy. For some reason, that night Clara doubted herself. She said, "I hope we sound okay." They tore it up. It was a $100-a-seat affair.

Mrs. Ward had gone to the Holy Land and came back with all this holy water. Rudy and I were at the door selling it in small vials. It was from the River Jordan. Mom asked, "Did you steal any of my water?" I broke out in a sweat. "No, Mom, I didn't take any of your holy water." I *had* taken a few dollars from the sales, but she made me feel so guilty, I slipped the money back into the box.

Mrs. Ward taught us how to pack a suitcase. We were allowed only one each when we traveled. She said, "You can get a closet full of clothes in one bag if you know how." We learned how to pack a car also. Before a show we would put on the shower and steam our clothes. We always stayed at the finest places. No dumps.

On the James Brown show at the Apollo we were the only Gospel group. James said that was the best show he had ever done. Herbie Moon and Ruth Bowen worked for the Queen Booking Agency. Ruth at the time was also booking Aretha Franklin. When Clara died, Herbie asked me if Willa was going to take over the group. I said, "Why don't you ask her yourself?" So he and Esther Ford came down from New York to see Willa. He was interested in booking her. Willa was doing nightclub work. I told him Willa has her own dynamite Gospel group. She's really good.

Herbie made the mistake of letting Mrs. Ward in on it, so she said, "Nobody is going to book any group called the Ward Singers unless it's me. I don't care who else wants to." Herbie booked us in Atlantic City to appear with the Clouds of Joy, but he got scared of Mom's threats to sue, so we didn't get to do the show. Herbie also booked us at the Bath House in New York, where Bette Midler got her start. Our group would have gone to the top, because the gays loved our singing. Herbie was going to book us with a famous white Gospel singing group and tour the South for big bucks, but that was never to be. Herbie Moon would have made the Willa Ward Singers as famous as the Ward Singers. Everybody wanted to work for Willa because they knew she was fair, but they were afraid of Mrs. Ward.

Clara and Mrs. Ward were living in the same neighborhood as the Jackson Five, Tina Turner and Ike Turner, Ray Charles, and people like that. She would belittle Willa's house, although it was very nice.

At Christmastime, Mrs. Ward would spare no expense with the lights and amplified music. She had so many lights it looked like daylight. One night I went to bed and woke up thinking it was the next day. I wondered why I was still tired. I had been sleeping only two hours, but the brightness made me think it was daytime. The music was all Ward Singers' records that came on at the same time each night and would stay on all night. The neighbors complained, so the city made her take the speakers down. People came from everywhere to see the Ward house. That was another thing the neighbors didn't like. All that traffic. The electric bill was tremendous, but they could afford it with all the money they were raking in. The Clara Ward Singers were booked solid.

Clara always wanted Willa to share in the good life, but she was torn between Mrs. Ward and Willa. Mrs. Ward was afraid Willa would influence her meal ticket.

It sure was a coincidence how the members of the Ward family died in bunches. When Mr. Ward died, three or four of them died right together. Then Clara and Willa's cousin Von Haskell Jones died on the 17th of September, James Burton on the 17th of October, and Mrs. Ward on the 27th of November. Rudy Scott was at her funeral. I could tell he was shook. He said Mrs. Ward had hexed him because he kept her kitchen set. The next month, on the 17th, Rudy died of a heart attack. I don't know if his own mind scared him to death or if Mom came back to get him. Every time I think of Rudy and the hex, I thank my lucky stars I put that holy water money back in the box.

I still get tearful when I think of Clara's death. I don't even like to talk about it. All I can say is, "I'm so sorry and I really miss her."

Appendix

The Ward Singers

Original Group: (a) Consecrated Gospel Singers; (b) Madam Gertrude Ward and Daughters
> Clara Ward
> Gertrude Ward
> Willa Ward

Ward Singers (early 1940s)
> Mrs. Booker
> Bernice Davis (pianist)
> Myrtle DeShields
> Florence Edwards (pianist)
> Gladys Gordon (pianist)
> Ruth Johnson
> Geraldine Keeys (pianist)
> Marie Millsap
> Luellen Price
> David Riddick (pianist)
> Mary Sample (pianist)
> Elizabeth Staples
> The Taylor Boys
> Catherine Thompson
> Clara Ward
> Gertrude Ward
> Willa Ward
> Louise Waters

Clara Ward Specials
> Lillie Davis
> Thelma Jackson
> Frances Johnson
> Frances Steadman

Note: We gratefully acknowledge the assistance of Anthony Heilbut, who catalogued all of the Wards' recordings.

Clara Ward Singers

       Gloria Berry

       Viola Crowley

       Freddie Daniels (pianist)

       Bernard Davis (pianist)

       Sylvester Dean (pianist/organist)

       Willie De John

       Bessie Griffin

       Alice Houston

       Agnes Jackson

       Celeste Jennings

       Geraldine Jones

       Anthony Lawson (pianist)

       Lillie Mae

       Charles May (pianist)

       Mildred Means

       Sandra Mitchell

       Betty Perkins

       Sandra Peyton

       Vermida Royster

       Adele Schofield

       Christine Stark

       Mavelyn Statham

       Madeline Thompson

       Clara Ward

       Willa Ward

       Alton Williams (pianist)

       John Wilson (pianist)

Famous Ward Singers (1947–1958)

       Edna Crockett

       Barry Currington (pianist)

       Esther Ford

       Ethel Gilbert

       Gloria Griffin

       Dorothy Holmes

       Thelma Jackson

Helen Johnson
Blanche Norton
Kitty Parham
Sandra Peyton
Marguerite Shaw (pianist)
Shirley Smith
Frances Steadman
Bobby Thompson (organist)
Madeline Thompson
Jessie Tucker
Henrietta Waddy
Clara Ward
Willa Ward
Carrie Williams
Marion Williams

Gertrude Ward Singers
Gloria Jean Berry
Edna Crocket
Adele Schofield Davis
Bernard Davis (pianist)
Dorothy Holmes
Alice Houston
Celeste Jennings
Helen Johnson
Vera Jones Kyler
Mildred Means
Sandra Mitchell
Miss Pat
Sandra Peyton
Marguerite Shaw
Madeline Thompson
Shirley Wahls
Tura Westbrook

Gertrude Ward Male Singers
Don Brown (musician)

Charles Coleman (musician)
Albert Goodson (musician)
George Hardcastle
Ira Harris (musician)
Carl Henry (musician)
Henry Jackson
Marvin Jenkins (musician)
Charles May
Daqienel Parks (musician)
David Piegon
Tyrone Scott (musician)
Sherwood Sledge
Raymond Smith
Charles Williams

Willa Ward Singers

Bobby Banks (organ)
Rita Bell (daughter)
Gloria Berry
Edna Crockett
Manrico Barry Currington (pianist)
Sticks Evans (drums)
Esther Ford
Helen Johnson
Arlene Mills
Rita Palmer
Sandra Peyton
Prince (pianist)
Helena Ruffin
Charlotte Sims (daughter)
Shirley Smith
Calvin Statham (pianist)
Madeline Thompson
Evelyn Vinson
Willa Ward
John Wilson (pianist)

Willa Moultrie Singers
Rita Bell
Helen Johnson
Shirley Smith
Madeline Thompson
Willa Ward

Gay Charmers
Della Jo Campbell
Jacqueline Casen
Doris Gibson
Leroy Lovett
    (pianist/arranger)
Willa Ward
Mary Wiley

Willettes
Vivian Dix
Doris Gibson
Blanche Norton
Dee Dee Sharp
Willa Ward
Mary Wiley

Willa Ward Trios
Rita Bell (drums)
Joe Gregory (bass)
Bruce Kareacher (bass)
Toni Rose (drums)
Willa Ward

Willa Ward Duo
Doris Gibson
Toni Rose
Willa Ward

Credits: Clara Ward, the Clara Ward Singers, and the Famous Ward Singers

Television Shows
>Danny Thomas
>Della Reese
>Dennis Morley
>Dial M for Music
>Dinah Shore
>Ed Sullivan
>Flip Wilson
>Hootenanny
>Horace Boyer Gospel Chronology Series
>Joey Bishop
>Johnny Carson
>Mike Douglas
>Monkees Special
>Playboy after Dark (Hugh Hefner)
>Robert Goulet Special
>Steve Allen
>Tennessee Ernie Ford
>Those Ragtime Years (Hoagy Carmichael)

Motion Pictures
>Spree (Universal, 1967)
>A Time to Sing (MGM, 1968)

Recordings
>(On BBS, Capitol, Columbia, Disneyland, Dot, Duke, Gotham, Nashboro, Nashville, Savoy, Spirit Feel, Vanguard, Verve, Ward, and Winset Records)

Selected Albums (* also singles)
>The Best of the Famous Ward Singers (Savoy 7015-DBL)
>Clara Ward Singers Greatest Hits (Winset PAS-21028)
>Clara Ward Tells Her Testimony in Church to Thousands in Sydney, Australia (Ward Records C Ward 101)

Evangelist Gertrude Ward: Journey to the Holy Land (Ward Records C Ward 201)

The Gospel Soul of Clara Ward (Nashboro 7098)

Gospel Warriors: Clara Ward (Spirit Feel SF 1003)

Hang Your Tears Out to Dry: Clara Ward (Verve V/V6/5002)

The Heart, the Faith, the Soul of Clara Ward (Verve 5019)

The Legendary Clara Ward Singers (Gold Castle True Believers D4-1H 71368-D21571 368)

*Lord Touch Me: Famous Ward Singers (Savoy 14006)

Madam Gertrude Ward Tells about Her Journey to the Holy Land (Ward Records G Ward 101)

Meetin' Tonight: Legendary Clara Ward Singers (Vanguard CD 19101 91351 VSD 2151)

Meeting Tonight: Famous Ward Singers (Savoy 14015)

Memorial Album: Famous Ward Singers (Savoy 14308)

A Merry Christmas with the Famous Ward Singers (Savoy MG14047)

Newport Spiritual All Stars: Famous Ward Singers (Savoy 14013)

*The Old Landmark: Famous Ward Singers (Savoy 14034)

*Packing Up: Famous Ward Singers (Savoy 14020)

Soul and Inspiration: Clara Ward (Capitol ST 126)

*Surely God Is Able: Famous Singers (Savoy 14001)

We Gotta Shout: Clara Ward and the Dukes of Dixieland (CL 2042/CS 8842)

The Whole World in His Hands: Famous Ward Singers (Savoy 14027)

Selected Singles

Clara Ward: How I Got Over (Gotham 674)

Clara Ward: Just over the Horizon (Savoy 14060)

Famous Ward Singers: Only the Crumbs (Savoy 4051B)

Famous Ward Singers: The Wonderful Counselor Is Pleading for Me (Savoy 4051B)

Gertrude Ward and Daughters: That Awful Day Will Surely Come (Savoy 4023A)

Ward Singers: I Feel the Holy Spirit (Savoy 14060)

Gold Records

How I Got Over: Clara Ward

Surely God Is Able: Famous Ward Singers

Other Singles (Savoy, numbers unavailable)

Anywhere in Glory

Are You Sure?

Bank in the Sky

Brighter Day

Climbing Jacob's Ladder

Come Ye Disconsolate

Day Is Past and Gone

Dry Bones

Farther On up the Road

Glory Glory to the King

God Moves in a Mysterious Way

Good News

Great Is the Lord

Great Judgment Morning

He Knows Just How Much You Can Bear

Hold Back the Tears

How Far Am I from Canaan

I Heard the Voice of Jesus Say

I Just Can't Make It by Myself

I Know It Was the Lord

I'll Anchor in the Harbor of the Lord

I'm Climbing Higher and Higher

I'm Climbing Higher Mountains

I'm Going Home

I'm Going There

I'm Gonna Use What I Got

In His Arms

I've Done My Work

I Want to Be More like Jesus

Jesus

Just over the Hill

Keep Your Hand on the Plow

King Jesus Is All I Need
Let the Train Roll Easy
Lord's Prayer
Move Along
Never Grow Old
Oh Gabriel
Oh Glory Hallelujah
Old Rugged Cross
Our God Is Real
Pay Day
Prayer Changes Things
Precious Lord
Prince of Peace
Pure Gold
Since I Found the Light
Sweet Little Jesus Boy
Swing Low, Sweet Chariot
This Little Light of Mine
Time Is Winding Up
Travelin' Shoes
Until I Found the Lord
Weeping May Endure for a Night
We Shall Be Changed
We're Gonna Have a Time
When I Get Home
When They Crown Him Lord of All
Who Shall Be Able to Stand?
Will the Circle Be Unbroken?
Will You Be There?

Colleges and Universities

East Stroudsburg State College, Stroudsburg, Pa.
Florida Presbyterian College, Lakeland, Fla.
Fort Valley State College, Fort Valley, Ga.
Geneva College, Beaver Falls, Pa.
Hope College, Holland, Mich.

St. Lawerence University, Canton, N.Y.
Staten Island Community College, N.Y.
University of California, Los Angeles, Calif.
University of Detroit, Mich.
Viterbo College, La Crosse, Wis.

Festivals

County Fair	Vallejo, Calif.
First International Jazz Festival	Washington, D.C.
German Jazz Festival	Essen, Germany
Hollywood Bowl	Hollywood, Calif.
Monterey Jazz Festival	Monterey, Calif.
Newport Jazz Festivals	Newport, R.I.
Paris Jazz Festival	Paris, France
Ravinia Festival	Chicago, Ill.
Santa Monica Jazz Festival	Santa Monica, Calif.
Shibe Park	Philadelphia, Pa.
Sydney Opera House	Sydney, Australia
Third Festival International	D'Antibes, France
Yankee Stadium	New York, N.Y.

Stage Shows

Apollo Theater	New York, N.Y.
Carnegie Hall	New York, N.Y.
Golden Horseshoe, Disneyland	Anaheim, Calif.
Gospel Highway, Apollo Theater	New York, N.Y.
Howard Theatre	Washington, D.C.
Jack Benny Show, Ziegfeld Theatre	New York, N.Y.
Johnny Holliday Show, Olympia Theatre	Paris, France
Lyndon B. Johnson Campaign Rally, Madison Square Garden	New York, N.Y.
Martin Luther King Rallies for Civil Rights	
Mitzi Gaynor Show, Gaynor Melody Land	Anaheim and San Carlos, Calif.
New Teatro Ferrocarritero	Mexico City, Mexico
O'Keefe Center	Toronto, Ont., Canada

Paramount Theater   Los Angeles, Calif.
Philharmonic Hall   New York, N.Y.
Tambourines to Glory,
   Little Theatre New York, N.Y.
Uptown Theatre   Philadelphia, Pa.
USO Tours Vietnam, Okinawa, Japan,
   Australia, Manila, Bangkok;
   Bob Hope/State Department

Other Engagements
   Supper Clubs
   Al Hirt's Club   New Orleans, La.
   Bitter End   New York, N.Y.
   Blue Angel   New York, N.Y.
   Cadillac Club   Philadelphia, Pa.
   Caesar's Palace   Las Vegas, Nev.
   Castaways   Miami Beach, Fla.
   Chevron Hotel   Sydney, Australia
   Copacabana   New York, N.Y.
   D'Amoto's   San Francisco, Calif.
   Desert Inn   Las Vegas, Nev.
   Embassy   Toronto, Ont., Canada
   Forty Thieves   Bermuda
   Havana Supper Club   Havana, Cuba
   Hotel Fremont   Las Vegas, Nev.
   Jazz Workshop   Boston, Mass.
   Lennon's Hotel   Brisbane, Australia
   London Palladium   London, England
   Marco Polo   Vancouver, B.C., Canada
   New Frontier   Las Vegas, Nev.
   Showboat   Philadelphia, Pa.
   Stardust Hotel   Las Vegas, Nev.
   Sugar Hill   San Franciso, Calif.
   Three European Tours   Scandinavia; India; Holland; Hawaii;
   London, England; Paris, France; Rome,
   Italy; Cairo, Egypt; Tangier, Morocco

Tivoli Gardens   Copenhagen, Denmark
Troubador   Los Angeles, Calif.
Village Vanguard   New York, N.Y.

Agents, Managers, and Bookers

Willard Alexander, New York, N.Y.
Associated Booking (Joe Glazer), New York, N.Y.
Associated Booking, Los Angeles, Calif.
Bob Bennet, Philadelphia, Pa.
Eastman Boomer, New York, N.Y.
Nick Botti, New York, N.Y.
John Hammond (manager)
Johnny Hyde
Monte Kay, New York and California
Bernie Landis
William Lobe, Los Angeles, Calif.
Lee Magid, California and New York
Queen Booking Agency (Herbie Moon), New York, N.Y.
Lee Rendi, Philadelphia, Pa.
Kal Ross (manager)
Bernie Rothbard, Philadelphia, Pa., and New York, N.Y.
Fred Strauss, Los Angeles, Calif.
Eddie Suez, Philadelphia, Pa.
Virginia Wicks (publicity), New York, N.Y.
William Morris Agency, New York, N.Y.

Songs and/or Arrangements Copyrighted by Clara Ward

Anywhere in Glory
Are You Sure?
Bank in the Sky
Brighter Day
Can You Find a Friend like Jesus?
Choose Your Seat and Sit Down
Climbing Jacob's Ladder
Come On
Come On Go with Me
Come to the Feast

Don't Give Up the Journey
Down by the Riverside (new matter)
Dry Bones (words and music adapted by Clara Ward)
From Youth to Old Age
Glory, Glory to the King
God Is Real
God Moves in a Mysterious Way
Good News
Great Is the Lord
Great Judgment Morning
He's Watching Over You
Hold Back the Tears
How I Got Over
I Feel the Holy Spirit
I Just Can't Make It by Myself
I Know It Was the Lord
I'll Anchor in the Harbor of the Lord
I'm Climbing Higher and Higher
I'm Climbing Higher Mountains
I'm Going Home
I'm Going There
I'm Gonna Use What I Got
I'm So Glad
I'm So Happy
In His Arms
In That Great Judgment Morning
In That Home By and By
In the Morning
I Promised the Lord
I Want to Be More like Jesus
Joshua Fit the Battle
Just over the Horizon
Keep Your Hand on the Plow
King Jesus Is All I Need
Let the Train Roll Easy
Lord Touch Me

Move Along
Neighbors
Never Grow Old
Oh, Gabriel
Oh, Glory Hallelujah
Oh, What a Wonderful Feeling
The Old Landmark
Only the Crumbs
Our God Is Real
Packing Up
Pay Day
Prince of Peace
Pure Gold
Run On
Since I Found the Light
Songs of the Reverend Herbert Brewster and Others (collection)
Special Songs of Clara Ward, Nos. 1, 2, 3, 4 (collections)
A Step to Make
Sweet Bye and Bye
Talk about Rain
There Is a Tree on Each Side of the River
This Little Light of Mine
Time Is Winding Up
Travelin' Shoes
Until I Found the Lord
Weeping May Endure for a Night
We'll Be Doing the Things We Love to Do
We'll Soon Be Done with Troubles and Trials
We're Gonna Have a Time
We Shall Be Changed
What Is Jesus to Me?
When I Get Home
When I Get Inside
When They Crown Him Lord of All
When We Get Up There
Who Is It?

Will the Circle Be Unbroken?
Will You Be There?
You Must Have Religion

Credits: Willa Ward and the Willa Ward Singers

Willa Ward Singers Engagements

The Barn	Cherry Hill, N.J.
Bolero	Wildwood, N.J.
Caesar's Boardwalk Regency	Atlantic City, N.J.
Chapel Hill University	Chapel Hill, N.C.
Coshockton Festival	Coshockton, Ohio
Crown and Anchor Inn	Provincetown, R.I.
Fort Valley College	Fort Valley, Ga.
Hampton University	Hampton, Va.
Henry's	Cherry Hill, N.J.
Latin Casino	Cherry Hill, N.J.
Le Bistro	Atlantic City, N.J.
Milwaukee Jazz Festival	Milwaukee, Wis.
Morehead State University	Morehead, Ky.
Philadelphia Folk Festival	Philadelphia, Pa.
Radio City Music Hall	New York, N.Y.
Reading Folk Festival	Reading, Pa.
Sands Supper Club	Toledo, Ohio
South Carolina State University	Orangeburg, S.C.
Temple University	Philadelphia, Pa.
Three Rivers	Syracuse, N.Y.
Tuskegee University	Tuskegee, Ala.
University of Wisconsin	Platteville, Wis.

Willa Ward Solo Engagements

Alpine Inn	Springfield, Pa.
Arthurs' Steak House	Philadelphia, Pa.
Asbourne Country Club	Philadelphia, Pa.

Baffa's	Manayunk, Pa.
Blue Moon Supper Club	Lewisburg, Pa.
Broadway Restaurant	Glenside, Pa.
Camp Williamsburg	Philadelphia, Pa.
Christopher's	Ambler, Pa.
Club 421	Philadelphia, Pa.
Club Martinique	Wildwood, N.J.
Colony	Philadelphia, Pa.
Drury Lane	Philadelphia, Pa.
Duke's Place	Lancaster, Pa.
DuPont Country Club	Wilmington, Del.
Embassy Supper Club	Philadelphia, Pa.
Gas Light	Philadelphia, Pa.
Hideaway	Cherry Hill, N.J.
Highland Inn	Jenkintown, Pa.
Holiday Inn	Philadelphia, Pa.
Holiday Inn	Wilkes-Barre, Pa.
Innflight Restaurants	Feasterville, Abington, and Willow Grove, Pa.
KNA Park Avenue Hotel	Oslo, Norway
Kronprins Herald (cruise ship)	Kiel, Germany
Lamplighter	Jenkintown, Pa.
Maggie's Pub	Philadelphia, Pa.
Mainland Inn	Mainland, Pa.
Mansion House	Philadelphia, Pa.
Marriott Hotel	Philadelphia, Pa.
Mastbaum Theatre (Harry Katz)	Philadelphia, Pa.
Maxine's	Philadelphia, Pa.
Miss Jeanne's Crossroad Tavern	Devon, Pa.
Nick Tally's	Atlantic City, N.J.
Not Quite Cricket (Latham Hotel)	Philadelphia, Pa.
Penthouse (with Earl Plummer)	Philadelphia, Pa.
Philmont Country Club	Philadelphia, Pa.
Queen Elizabeth II (cruise ship)	London, England
RDA Club	Philadelphia, Pa.
SAS Scandinavian Hotel	Bergen, Norway

Saxony East   Philadelphia, Pa.
Sheraton Hotel   Fort Washington, Pa.
Sheraton Hotel   Washington, D.C.
Sportsman Club   Philadelphia, Pa.
Three Chefs   Bala-Cynwyd, Pa.
Three Rivers Inn   Syracuse, New York
Twadells   Paoli, Pa.
Twenty-One Key Club   Philadelphia, Pa.
Two Tour Club   Philadelphia, Pa.
Venus Lounge   Philadelphia, Pa.
William Penn Inn   Gwynedd, Pa.
Wooden Indian Holiday Inn   Perrysburg, Ohio
Yorktown Inn   Jenkintown, Pa.

Willa Ward Duo and Trio Engagements

Avalon Supper Club   Hazleton, Pa.
Christopher's   Ambler, Pa.
Club 86   Geneva, N.Y.
Club Zanzibar   Toronto, Ont., Canada
Edge Supper Club   Philadelphia, Pa.
Guildwood Inn   Sarnia, Ont., Canada
King's Room   Saratoga, N.Y.
Le Moyne Manor   Syracuse, N.Y.
Millers Supper Club   Shamokin, Pa.
Phil's Restaurant   Lake George, N.Y.
Rube's   Allentown, Pa.
Shell Bar   Oahu, Hawaii
Spotted Hog   Lahaska, Pa.
Troia Steak House   Madison, Wis.
Trolley Stop   Skippack, Pa.
Tropical Inn   Kingston, N.Y.
Village Bar   Lancaster, Pa.
William Penn Inn   Gwynedd, Pa.

Gay Charmers Engagements

Adelphia's Auditorium

(United Civic Organization)   Philadelphia, Pa.
Black Orchid   Montreal, Que., Canada
Citizens' Club   Devon, Pa.
Over the Top   Merchantville, N.J.
Supper Club   Red Bank, N.J.
Town Hall (Cable Tow Square Club)   Philadelphia, Pa.
VPA Supper Club   Philadelphia, Pa.

Gay Charmers/Willettes Recordings (singles)

Dance Du Du Du Dance: Gay Charmers (Savoy)
Get In and Shut the Door: Gay Charmers (Swan 4032A)
Groovy Shoes: Gay Charmers (Savoy)
Honky Tonk: Gay Charmers (Moultrie Records)
One Love Lost: Willettes (Jamie J-WET 2)
Summertime Is Gone: Willettes (Jamie J-WET 1)
Walk beside Him: Gay Charmers (Savoy S-W-W 70280)
What Can I Do: Gay Charmers (Swan 4032B)
Why Darling: Gay Charmers (Savoy S-W-W 70280)

Recording Artists for Whom Willettes Sang Background

Frankie Avalon
Freddie Cannon
Chubby Checker
Christine Clark
Nicky Dimatteo
Dion
Fabian
Screamin' Jay Hawkins
Louis Jordan
Patti LaBelle
Bobby Rydell
Dee Dee Sharp

Original Songs Written and Recorded by Willa Ward Moultrie and Company

Clinging Vine (music: John Moultrie and Willa Ward Moultrie;
    words: Mary Wiley)

Dance Du Du Du Dance (music: Willa Ward Moultrie; words: Doris Gibson and Della Jo Campbell)

Groovy Shoes (John Moultrie, Willa Ward Moultrie, and Doris Gibson)

Thrill Me, Baby (Willa Ward Moultrie, John Moultrie, Leroy Lovett, Della Jo Campbell, and Doris Gibson)

What Can I Do? (Willa Ward Moultrie, Leroy Lovett, Doris Gibson, John Moultrie, and Della Jo Campbell)

Who Shall Be Able to Stand? (Willa Ward)

Why Darling (Willa Ward Moultrie)

Honors and Tributes

The Wards and the Singers

1953, 1954, 1955	*Pittsburgh Courier* Award to Ward Singers as "World's Best Singers of Gospel"
1954	City of Philadelphia Citation to Ward Singers on their twenty-first anniversary
1957	"Best Singers of the Twentieth Century" Trophy to Ward Singers at the Abyssinian Baptist Church (Rep. Adam Clayton Powell Jr., Pastor) annual awards event: "The Ward Singers have given something to God's music and to His Gospel that has echoed around the world." Others receiving awards included Thurgood Marshall (Man of the Century), Mahalia Jackson, Sugar Ray Robinson, and Marguerite Belafonte (Woman of the Year).
1959	Interurban League's Junior Oscar Award to Gay Charmers as "person or persons who most advanced American music during the year"
1967	Hollywood Overseas Committee, USO, Commendation to Clara Ward:

January 4, 1967

Dear Miss Ward,

On behalf of the Hollywood Overseas Committee, the U.S.O. and the Department of Defense, I wish to express our gratitude to you and the Clara Ward Singers for your recent Vietnam tour.

The outstanding contribution you made to the morale of our troops is best reflected in the appreciative reports and letters I have received in your praise from both enlisted men and officers.

We are all very proud of your group and we join with all the service men and women you met and entertained in saying, "Thank You—and we salute you."

Sincerely,

Chairman

GEORGE CHANDLER

1967   Department of Defense, Certificate of Esteem to Clara Ward:

The Department of The Army

Washington, D.C. 20710

January 25, 1967

Dear Miss Ward,

I take great pleasure in transmitting to you the enclosed certificate of esteem which has been awarded by the Department of Defense. This certificate is presented in gratitude for your entertainment tour of Armed Forces Installations in Vietnam.

Entertainment from home is extremely popular with our service men and women throughout the world and is among the most effective of the recreational programs designed to stimulate and maintain morale in the Armed Services.

It is hoped that this certificate of esteem will serve in some measure to express the deep appreciation of the Department of Defense for your generous contribution to this program.

Sincerely,

STANLEY R. RESOR

Secretary of the Army

1974 Songwriters' Hall of Fame, posthumous induction ceremony for Clara Ward

1981 Operation PUSH (People United to Save Humanity) memorial tributes to Clara Ward (1924–73) and Gertrude Ward (1901–81), presented by Mayor Richard Hatcher (board chairman) and the Reverend Jesse L. Jackson (national president)

1985 Gospel Music Association, posthumous induction of Clara Ward into the Gospel Music Hall of Fame, Nashville, Tennessee, paying tribute to her for "the accomplishments and spirit of selfless dedication that have touched the lives of millions through the spreading of the True Word and the Good News" in music and her "indelible impact on the annals of gospel history."

1986 Diane Brown at Heavenly Hall, tribute to Willa Ward for her contribution to Gospel music

1988 Uppre Inc. B.G. Hall of Fame Award for "Outstanding Achievement in Gospel Music"

1992 Philadelphia City Council Citation to the Ward Singers: "The council notes that the Ward singers have inspired countless thousands of people in this country, Europe, the Holy Land, and the Orient. Their music transcends age, race, and religion. Their concerts are sold out, their recordings sell in the millions, and still the faithful come to be entertained by this remarkable group." (Each singer received a trophy and citation with name inscribed. Others receiving awards were Gospel pioneers the Dixie Hummingbirds, Angelic Gospel Singers, and the Reverend Charles A. Tindley.)

1992 Faith Tabernacle Mutchmore Memorial Baptist Church Trophy (given by Gladys Bond and the Reverend C. W. Ashe II, Pastor) to Willa Ward-Royster for continued service in the field of Gospel music

1992 Horace Clarence Boyer,in his Gospel chronology radio series, honored the Ward Singers and interviewed Willa Ward as their spokesperson.

1992   Philadelphia Music Alliance Fifth Annual Awards, ceremony
            honoring Clara Ward and the Famous Ward Singers. Willa
            Ward, accompanied at her request by Marion Williams,
            Kitty Parham, Frances Steadman, Esther Ford, and
            Marguerite Shaw, accepted in their name. A plaque
            embedded in the sidewalk on the Avenue of the Arts in
            Center City, Philadelphia, joins those of Pearl Bailey, Ethel
            Waters, Mario Lanza, Patti LaBelle, Marian Anderson, the
            Dixie Hummingbirds, John Coltrane, Eugene Ormandy,
            Jeanette MacDonald, and many others.

1994   Gospel Music Preservation Alliance, Inc., Serena Blanca,
            President, Certificate of Appreciation to Willa Ward-
            Royster

1994   Bernice Johnson Reagon of the Smithsonian Institution,
            on the Wade in the Water radio series paid tribute to
            Clara Ward and the Ward Singers.

1994   *Hallelujah Mahalia* by Donald Welsh, a musical chronicling
            the life of Mahalia Jackson (presented at the Philadelphia
            Ethical Society building), included Ward Singers hits that
            brought audiences to their feet at every performance

1994,   Stellar Award from Johnny Lloyd's "Gospel Music of the
1995,   Masters" Series
1996

1995   James Cleveland Award for "Outstanding Contribution in
            Gospel Music" to Clara Ward Singers on Gospel Music
            Stellar Awards television show

N.D.   *The Gospel Music Encyclopedia*, by Robert Anderson and Gail
            North, listing for Clara Ward

Tribute to Marion Williams

Marion Williams (August 1927–July 1994) "took a simple line and
   infused the spirit of all humanity with awesome deliverance. Her
   readings of gospel standards and spirituals grabbed the listener
   with an intensity never before experienced. Perhaps only Mahalia
   and Clara could expel such heavenly magnificence with such
   mortal power and passion. . . . Let the light shine on Marion"
   (Wayne Trujillo, Minturn, Colo.)

Accolades bestowed on Marion Williams in the last year of her life:

August 8, 1993	The McArthur "Genius Award" (and cash grant of $375,000) for outstanding service to the community
December 6, 1993	One of the Kennedy Center Honors, presented to living artists for lifetime achievement. The other recipients on this occasion were Johnny Carson, Arthur Mitchell, Sir George Solti, and Stephen Sondheim
April 30, 1994	Philadelphia Music Alliance Award and sidewalk plaque on the Avenue of the Arts presented to Marion Williams as a member of the Ward Singers

Index

13.56   3/02/01